25°

Political Islam in Southeast Asia: Moderates, Radicals and Terrorists

Angel M. Rabasa

ADELPHI PAPER 358

Oxford University Press, Great Clarendon Street, Oxford OX2 6DP
Oxford New York
Athens Auckland Bangkok Bombay Calcutta Cape Town
Dar es Salaam Delhi Florence Hong Kong Istanbul Karachi
Kuala Lumpur Madras Madrid Melbourne Mexico City Nairobi
Paris Taipei Tokyo Toronto
and associated companies in Ibadan

Oxford is a trade mark of Oxford University Press

Published in the United States
by Oxford University Press Inc., New York

© The International Institute for Strategic Studies 2003

First published May 2003 by **Oxford University Press** for
The International Institute for Strategic Studies
Arundel House, 13–15 Arundel Street, Temple Place, London WC2R 3DX
www.iiss.org

Director John Chipman
Editor Tim Huxley
Copy Editor Matthew Foley
Production Shirley Nicholls, Simon Nevitt

British Library Cataloguing in Publication Data
Data available

Library of Congress Cataloguing in Publication Data

ISBN 0-19-852911-2
ISSN 0567-932x

Contents

Tables and Figures

Introduction

Events since 11 September 2001 have dramatically altered the political environment in the Muslim world, and in Southeast Asia in particular. The divide has sharpened between the West and its secular values and institutions and the world of militant Islam and, within the Muslim world, between moderates and radicals. This paper examines trends in Southeast Asian Islam over the last two decades, the impact of the US-led war on terrorism and the policies that Southeast Asian governments, the US and other Western countries could pursue to strengthen moderate and tolerant tendencies within Southeast Asian Islam.

The US-led war on terrorism has coincided with, and is in some ways an effect of, an upsurge in Islamic self-awareness and political activism in the Muslim world. Denoted 'Islamisation', this has manifested itself in greater religiosity; greater insistence on the outward displays of piety; greater social distance between the sexes; overt concern with Islamic dietary restrictions; intolerance of un-Islamic public behaviour; exclusive, identity-driven politics; and, in some cases, political extremism and a propensity for violence.[1] In non-Arab countries, Islamisation has involved the importation of Arab-origin ideology and religious practices, greetings, terminology and even mosque architecture. This Arabisation process has polarised Islam in Southeast Asia. Here, the cultural context is quite different from the Arab world, with a more moderate and tolerant practice of Islam than in the Islamic heartland of the Middle East.

An important distinction separating the different strains within political Islam is between those who advocate an Islamic state, and those who are willing to accept a secular one. Yet while radical Islamists seek to establish an Islamic economy and political order, there is in fact a great deal of disagreement about what constitutes an Islamic state. The most authoritative Islamic scripture, the Koran, the *hadith* and the *sunnah* (the tradition of the Prophet Muhammad), provide general principles of governance, but no specific blueprint.[2] Among modern self-defined Islamic states, there are significant differences between Iran, where clerical supremacy over the political authorities is firmly entrenched, and Saudi Arabia, Pakistan or Sudan, which follow the Sunni tradition of rulers governing in consultation with, but not subordinate to, the clerical establishment.

It is possible to make further distinctions between those Islamist parties and movements that operate within the established political system, and those that operate outside it. The latter includes terrorist groups such as the Jemaah Islamiyah and armed militants such as the Kumpulan Militan Malaysia (KMM) and Indonesia's Laskar Jihad and Laskar Jundullah. While Islamic radicals in Southeast Asia are a small minority within the region's Muslim communities, they constitute a serious threat to stability and provide the support network that allows international terrorist groups to operate.

Islamists by and large reject nationalism and manifest pan-Islamic aspirations. Islam considers all Muslims brethren, linked by bonds that transcend man-made distinctions. Nationalism, moreover, is regarded as *asabiyyah* (sectarianism), contaminated by Western secularism and involving loyalties superseding loyalty to God. Conversely, nationalism in many parts of the Islamic world has employed a Muslim idiom and has proved an effective unifying force among Muslims opposing Western domination. In its most radical expression, pan-Islamism calls for the re-establishment of the caliphate – the institution of the successor of the Prophet and supreme head of the Muslim community. The caliphate was formally abolished by the Turkish Republic in 1924 after the downfall of the Ottoman Sultanate.[3]

The regional strategies of such groups differ in important ways. The Hizbal-Tahrir claims that it favours a peaceful *jihad* – that is, spreading Islam through persuasion and conversion rather than violence – but the group has been involved in terrorism and subversive activities in Egypt and Jordan and has been outlawed throughout the Middle East and Central Asia. In Indonesia, in contrast, it appears to have moderated its stance, and the authorities have not regarded it as a threat.[4]

Radical groups in Southeast Asia such as the regional Jemaah Islamiyah organisation and some Philippine and Thai Muslim separatists reject the legitimacy of the nation-state and aspire to establish a pan-Islamic state encompassing Indonesia, Malaysia, the Muslim areas of the Philippines and Thailand and, eventually, Singapore and Brunei. They also profess to see their struggle as part of a global contest between Islam and the West. A large sector of political Islam has taken an anti-Western and anti-American cast. This is commonly explained by reference to US support for Israel in the Israeli–Palestinian conflict, and more generally by US and Western backing for a regional status quo that is perceived as unjust. Certainly, the Palestinian problem is a neuralgic issue, particularly but not exclusively in the Arab regions of the Muslim world. But this anger has deeper roots in the trauma of the Islamic world's encounter with modernity. It is directed at the US, the mainstay of the international order that the radicals oppose. As the chief agent of global economic, political and social change, the US represents the forces and values that, in the view of some Muslims, threaten Muslim societies and values.

The external sources of Islamic radicalism

Islamic radicalism in Southeast Asia has both external and domestic sources. The interplay of the two produces the specific characteristics of each of the national variants. The underlying external source is the radical change that the Muslim world has undergone in modern times. Factors such as globalisation and the intrusion of Western culture, together with changes in the social and economic structures of Muslim countries, have created the conditions for a religious resurgence.

Against this background, a number of specific events have acted as catalysts for the rise of radical political Islam in the Muslim world in general, and in Southeast Asia in particular. The first was the Islamic revolution in Iran in 1979. Political movements challenged the West from an Islamic perspective from the earliest days of Western domination of the Muslim world; the Muslim Brotherhood and other Islamic revivalist organisations were founded in the 1920s, for example. But the most important opposition in the immediate post-colonial period came from secular forces, such as Nasser's Arab socialism, the Ba'ath party of Syria and Iraq, the Algerian National Liberation Front and Sukarno's idiosyncratic blend of ideologies in

Indonesia. However, these regimes and ideologies failed to fulfill their promises of economic growth, social justice and international strength. Their appeal was on the wane even before the ousting of the Shah unleashed new and more dangerous forces.

The Iranian revolution demonstrated that religious fundamentalists could overthrow an apparently strong secular government – and one supported by the US – and establish in its place a state with an exclusive Islamic identity. Yet the clerical government in Iran is a Khomeinist innovation, not a natural outgrowth of Shi'ite Islam. Khomeini and his supporters could only take power after fundamentally distorting the Shi'ite doctrine that all worldly authority was to be opposed by Shi'ite believers until the return of the Twelfth Imam. The keystone of the Khomeinist state, the *velayat-e-faqih* (guardianship of the jurist), was rejected by Shi'ite traditionalists as a fabrication inspired by Egyptian Sunnis. Khomeini prevailed because he and the revolutionaries controlled the levers of power and were able to silence their opponents.[5]

The second catalyst was the spread of Islamic fundamentalism, particularly the Saudi Wahhabi variant. Although the doctrine of Wahhabism dates back to the eighteenth century and has been the official interpretation of Islam in Saudi Arabia since the establishment of the monarchy in the 1920s, the export of religious fundamentalism increased after the 1973 Arab oil embargo. The steep rise in oil prices gave the Saudis the means to fund the expansion of religious outreach activities. Following the takeover by religious dissidents of the Grand Mosque in Mecca in November 1979, the Saudis tightened religious observances at home and stepped up the export of fundamentalist doctrine through an aggressive proselytising campaign, stretching from Bosnia to the Philippines. They funded mosques, Islamic boarding schools (*madrassa*) and Islamic social welfare organisations which, in countries such as Pakistan, filled the void left by ineffectual or non-existent state institutions. These proselytising activities dovetailed with the movements for mass religious education in the Muslim world that began in the 1950s, but whose effects were not fully felt until the 1980s.[6]

The impact of Middle Eastern finance is also important in the radicalisation of Southeast Asian Muslims. There are considerable financial links between the Middle East and Southeast Asia, and the obstacles to the flow of funds to extremist and terrorist organisations are weak. With the exception of Singapore, banking and financial systems across the region are poorly regulated. Moreover, there is widespread use of the unregulated system of remittances and currency exchange known as *hawalah*, which involves no physical or electronic transfer of funds, and leaves little or no record of transactions. As a result, the system is almost impenetrable to financial or law-enforcement authorities.

The third catalyst was the Afghan war against the Soviets, which attracted militants from all over the Muslim world during the 1980s. While by and large they were devout Muslims themselves, the Afghan fighters saw their struggle as a national liberation war as well as a religious conflict. For the foreign *mujahideen*, however, the Afghan war was purely and simply a *jihad*, coextensive with other battlefields in Kashmir, Chechnya, Bosnia or Mindanao. A large number of 'Afghanis' or veterans of the Afghan war play key roles in terrorist and armed radical Islamic movements throughout the Muslim world. The Afghan conflict served not only as the training ground for today's Islamic terrorists and radicals, but also provided the context for the creation of the transnational networks that served as the conduit for al-Qaeda operations.

The domestic sources of Islamic radicalism

Some trends and developments are specific to Southeast Asia. The deterioration of economic and social conditions after the 1997–98 economic crisis produced an environment favourable to the activities of political and religious extremists. These domestic factors interacted with broader external trends to produce greater Islamic militancy in the region.

In Indonesia, the principal factor was the weakening of state authority after President Suharto's resignation in 1998, although the Islamic resurgence actually began in the latter years of his presidency, when he sought to mobilise support among Muslims by presenting himself as a defender of their interests. The downfall of the New Order regime sharpened competition among political sectors, some of which saw Islam as a path to political power. The political disorder also produced tactical alliances between élite and military factions and Islamic extremists, which gave the extremists greater scope to expand their political influence. Radical militias and armed vigilante groups made their appearance in connection with the outbreak of communal conflict in Maluku in 2000. These groups engaged in armed struggle against Christians there and in Sulawesi, and more widely in the suppression of what they considered un-Islamic activities. They justified their violence with allegations that the authorities in Jakarta had failed to protect Muslim interests, but their larger goal was to weaken Indonesia's moderate Muslim and secular forces and press a radical Islamist political agenda.[7]

In Malaysia, the key factor was competition between the dominant political grouping, the United Malays National Organisation (UMNO), and the Islamic fundamentalist opposition party, the Pan-Malay Islamic Party (PAS). Since, aside from language, the defining characteristic of the Malay people is the Muslim religion, political competition between UMNO and PAS revolved around the promotion of ethno-religious interests. This dynamic gradually shifted the goal posts in the fundamentalists' favour. UMNO's efforts to give Islam a greater role in society allowed PAS to trump UMNO by offering a more thoroughgoing Islamic programme.

In the southern Philippines and southern Thailand, militancy among Muslims manifests itself as resistance to central government. In the Philippines, demographic changes have altered the ethnic and religious balance in the south, from an overall Muslim majority in Mindanao and the Sulu archipelago at the end of the nineteenth century to less than one-fifth of the population today. These changes precipitated bitter conflicts over land distribution and ownership and generated a strong sense of grievance on the part of the Muslim population. A separatist Muslim insurgency was launched in the early 1970s and, with various permutations, persists to this day. In Thailand, separatism among ethnic Malays in the southern provinces reflected resentment of earlier Thai governments' assimilationist policies and anger at the relative lack of opportunities for participation in the country's political and economic life. In these cases, as in Chechnya and Kashmir, religious identity coincides with ethnic identity and even social status to the extent that it is difficult to determine whether religion is fundamental in explaining the rebellions, or whether it only reinforces other, more compelling factors.

Chapter 1

The varieties of Islam in Southeast Asia

Southeast Asia is the cultural as well as the geographic crossroads of Asia, where Sinic, Hindu, Islamic and Western civilisations have met and interacted for almost a millennium. A far from homogenous Muslim arc stretches from southern Thailand through the Malay peninsula, Sumatra, Java, parts of Kalimantan (Borneo) and Sulawesi, to the Sulu archipelago and Mindanao in the southern Philippines; there are Christian, animist or mixed communities in Maluku, Sulawesi, Borneo, the Nusa Tenggara islands of Indonesia and Papua; a Hindu majority in Bali; a predominantly Catholic population in the Philippines; diverse cultures, largely Theravada Buddhist, in mainland Southeast Asia; and ethnic Chinese communities throughout the region. Peninsular or western Malaysia is home to large ethnic Chinese and Hindu minorities. Indigenous people such as Dayaks and Kadazan, mostly animist or Christian, constitute the majority in eastern Malaysia (Sarawak and Sabah). In Indonesia, although non-Muslims number only around 12% of the population, they constitute majorities in several provinces in the centre and east (see Table 1 on the next page).

Islam was brought to Southeast Asia by Arab, Persian and Indian traders and spread largely through the conversion of élites; thus, it developed under different conditions from other regions in the Muslim world, where the religion was established through Arab or Turkish conquest. In Southeast Asia, the continuity of élites under the new religious dispensation permitted the preservation of strong pre-Islamic elements. By the end of the thirteenth century, the new religion had become entrenched in the Malay peninsula and Sumatra, and spread throughout the region from the fourteenth to the seventeenth centuries.

Table 1 **Religious composition of Central and Eastern Indonesia**

	Muslims (%)	Christians (%)	Other (%)
East Kalimantan	85.68	13.55	0.77
Central Kalimantan	69.91	18.39	11.70
West Kalimantan	56.34	30.18	13.48
South Kalimantan	96.75	1.37	1.88
North Sulawesi	44.10	52.00	3.90
Central Sulawesi	76.23	19.42	4.35
South Sulawesi	88.50	9.70	1.80
Southeast Sulawesi	96.27	2.42	1.31
West Nusa Tenggara	95.90	1.00	3.10
East Nusa Tenggara*	9.12	86.05	4.83
Maluku	56.79	42.70	0.51
Papua	15.00	83.00	2.00

Note: *Includes the now-independent East Timor.
Sources: 'Indonesian Provinces of EAGA (East ASEAN Growth Area)',
www.brunet.bn/org/bimpeabc/Idprov.htm; and 'The Indonesian Provinces',
www.indonesia-ottawa.org/indonesia/provinces.

Islam in Southeast Asia is not only uneven in its geographical contiguity, but also extraordinarily diverse internally. This reflects the region's cultural, ethnic and linguistic diversity and the presence of substantial non-Muslim communities, which by and large have accustomed Muslims in Southeast Asia to coexistence with other religious and cultural traditions. Although there are common themes, the interaction between Islam and political, ethnic and territorial issues unfolds differently from country to country, region to region, island to island.

The complexity of Islam in Indonesia

In Indonesia, degrees of Islamic observance range from orthodox fundamentalism in Aceh to the more diluted form of Islam known as *kejawen* in parts of Java. In eastern and central Java, the majority of Muslims are traditionalists, a tendency that incorporates strong elements of Sufi mysticism and pre-Islamic Javanese traditions far removed in form and spirit from Wahhabi severity and intolerance. Traditionalists are represented by Nahdlatul Ulama ('Awakening of the Religious Scholars'), the largest social-welfare organisation in the Muslim world with a claimed membership of over 40 million people.

The organisation was founded in 1926 by a group of *kiai* (traditional Islamic teachers) alarmed by the inroads made by modernists. It cooperated with the nationalists in the struggle for independence against the Dutch from 1945 to 1949. In the interest of national unity, its leaders agreed that independent Indonesia was not to be organised as an Islamic state. Nahdlatul Ulama participated in elections until 1984, when it abandoned formal political activity and rededicated itself to religious, social and cultural activities.

Although representing traditionalist Islam, the Nahdlatul Ulama leadership has endeavoured to adapt to modern conditions. Under the chairmanship of Abdurrahman Wahid (president of Indonesia in 1999–2001), the curriculum in the Nahdlatul Ulama *pesantren* (Islamic boarding schools) was reformed and secular subjects added. The leadership also worked through associated foundations and research institutes to promote a democratic civil society and reconcile Islam and nationalism. Nahdlatul Ulama tends not to identify non-Muslims as the source of Muslims' problems, and is hospitable to inter-faith dialogue and cooperation.[1] Its former chairman Abdurrahman Wahid, also known as Gus Dur, is a founding member of the Shimon Peres Peace Foundation.

The second important tendency within Indonesian Islam is modernism, which aims to 'purify' Islam from 'heterodox' practices. Modernists are largely drawn from among the urban population and professionals. The founders of Muhammadiyah, established in 1912 as the institutional expression of the Indonesian modernist movement, wanted to banish 'superstition', for example some of the practices associated with traditionalist Indonesian Islam. Their model of education was the Dutch school system with the inclusion of religious subjects, and they stressed the primacy of rational thinking (*ijtihad*) as opposed to blind obedience to the traditional *ulama*.[2] The Dutch system was also the main source of inspiration for the replacement of the Middle Eastern model of religious education by influential Islamic education institutions such as the Institut Agama Islam Negeri (IAIN – the State Institute for Islamic Studies).[3]

Indonesian modernists believe in adjusting *sharia* (Islamic law) to current conditions. Thus, Muhammadiyah chairman Ahmad Syafii Maarif has criticised Acehnese militants for 'simplifying' *sharia* by seeking to enforce *jilbab* (Muslim headscarves) for women and *rajam* (death by stoning) for adulterers. In Maarif's view, Islamic law needs to be reformed since in many cases it is no longer relevant.[4] A more pluralistic interpretation is advanced by respected scholar Nurcholish Madjid, who argues that those who want to insert *sharia* into the Indonesian constitution do not have a proper understanding of it. According to Madjid, every individual can design their own *sharia*. Attempts to impose it on the state are doomed to failure.[5]

Indonesia has not proved to be fertile soil for Wahhabism. The Padri movement in western Sumatra in the 1820s and 1830s was Wahhabi-inspired, but did not leave a lasting impression. At its foundation, Muhammadiyah was influenced by conservative but less extreme Salafi teachings.[6] The Muslim Brotherhood took root in Indonesia, but now stands for toleration. More recently, Saudi foundations have been active in Indonesia. The Rabita al-Alam al-Islami, a Saudi non-governmental organisation (NGO), funds about 180 Indonesian institutions. The Suharto government tried to control Saudi money by making it compulsory for funds to be channelled through the Ministry of Religious Affairs, but this no longer appears to be the case.

Islamic extremism in Indonesia has been associated with clerics of Arab origin: Laskar Jihad leader Ja'afar Umar Thalib, Jemaah Islamiyah founders Abu Bakar Bashir and Abdullah Sungkar and Front Pembela Islam (Islam Defenders Front) head Muhammad Habib Rizieq, for example. The Arab community was influential in religious affairs during the Dutch colonial period, but was eclipsed during the republican period by indigenous *ulama*. The dislocations brought about by the fall of the New Order and the emergence of radical Islamic groups provided opportunities for Arab-Indonesians to reassert themselves and gain political influence. The two major Arab-Indonesian organisations, the Jamiat Kahir and al-Irshad, both have moderate political agendas. That said, there is considerable evidence that Middle Eastern influences have shaped the ideology of most, if not all, of Indonesia's militant movements.

The fusion of religion and ethnicity in Malaysia

As in Indonesia, Islam in Malaysia was deeply influenced by 'traditional' practices and beliefs derived from Hinduism and animism. From the seventeenth century onwards, returning scholars from the Arabian peninsula and Egypt introduced a more *sharia*-oriented or scriptural interpretation of Islam. In modern times, Islam in Malaysia has become more homogeneous and orthodox. The development of a centralised religious authority to oversee Islamic affairs in the Malay States began under the British. *Sharia* and *adat* (customary law) were codified and subordinated to the British legal code and the enactments of the colonial administration. Religious officials were engaged as government functionaries at state level. After Malaysia's independence in 1957, the constitution gave the country's nine sultans the final say in matters relating to religion.[7] The result was enforced Sunni orthodoxy. Heterodox religious movements, largely tolerated in Indonesia, were suppressed in Malaysia as 'cults'. In 1994, for instance, the government banned a major Islamic movement, Darul Arqam, accused of spreading deviationist teachings. The movement's goal was to implement a wholly Islamic way of life, though it had also criticised the government and the established religious authorities.[8] Darul Arqam was also controversial in Indonesia, but the decision to ban it was left to provincial prosecutors.[9]

The ethnic composition of Malaysian society is another factor in the country's religio-political development. Malays, the politically dominant ethnic group, constitute only a little over 50% of the population. The other main sections comprise ethnic Chinese (24%), Indians (8%) and non-Malay indigenous groups.[10] Political insecurity has produced a greater insistence on ethnic and religious solidarity, reinforced by the status of Islam as a pillar of Malay identity. In Indonesia, by contrast, Muslims make up some 88% of the population, and national identity is defined in non-religious terms.[11]

A third factor strongly influencing Malaysian Islam is the *dakwah* movement (literally 'the call'), which promotes a return to orthodox Islam. Traditional beliefs in spirits and magic rituals still persist among rural Malays, but have been attenuated by Islamic propagation.[12] Muslim organisations in Malaysia engage in two kinds of *dakwah* activities: one is Islamic education for their members, the other propagation of Islam and Islamic practices to the public at large.[13] Islamic religious education comprises, at the elementary school level, an informal network of *madrassa*, some of them reportedly funded by the Saudis. Islamic education received a strong impulse in the consolidation of Malay political consciousness that followed ethnic riots in Kuala Lumpur in 1969. Although the level of militancy in the Malaysian Islamic education system has never approached that of

Pakistan, it nevertheless has sustained fundamentalist politico-religious movements.

Muslims in Singapore

Muslims constitute about 15% of the population of Singapore. For the most part they are ethnic Malays, though there are also small minorities of Indian and Pakistani origin. Malays have been an important component of the Singaporean population since the establishment of the British settlement by Sir Stamford Raffles. Raffles set aside the Kampong Glam area for Sultan Hussein Shah and his followers, recognised Hussein, an unsuccessful claimant to the sultanate of Johor, as sultan and secured a treaty that gave the British the right to establish a trading post on the island. A new treaty in 1824 conceded to the British East India Company full sovereignty over Singapore. In 1826, the Company's holdings in Singapore, Malacca and Penang were consolidated into one administrative entity, the Straits Settlements. By the 1830s, Singapore had become the most important trading city in Southeast Asia, with a European administration and a multiethnic but mainly ethnic Chinese population.

Throughout the period of British rule, the ethnic components of Singapore remained separate communities, with their own languages, religions and ways of life. With the onset of decolonisation, the issue of political control raised tensions between the Chinese and Malay communities, both within Singapore and in the Malaysian Federation, of which Singapore was a part between 1963 and 1966, and there were serious communal riots in Singapore in 1964. Since then, Prime Minister Lee Kuan Yew's People's Action Party (PAP) has endeavoured to build an ethnically inclusive society. The government ensures that all ethnic communities are adequately represented in parliament, and promotes inter-communal contacts through educational and social institutions.[14]

Malay Muslims are overwhelmingly Sunni, and adhere to the Shafi'ite school of Islamic jurisprudence. The administration of Muslim religious affairs is regulated by a 1966 law, which established the Majlis Ugama Islam Singapura (Singapore Islamic Religious Council) to administer the collection of Muslim tithes (*zakat*) and charitable trusts (*wakaf*); supervise the construction and administration of mosques and *madrassa*; issue *fatwah* on points of religious law; and manage the *hajj* (the pilgrimage to Mecca). The members of the Council are nominated by Muslim societies and appointed by the president of Singapore. The Council advises the president on all things relating to Muslim affairs.

The unique entity of Brunei Darussalam

Brunei is a unique political entity in Southeast Asia, in some ways the remnant of an earlier era. The sultan is the absolute ruler, and also the head of Islam. The official version of the religion is Sunni Islam and, as with all Malays, the Shafi'ite school of jurisprudence. Other interpretations are tolerated, but not the propagation of heterodox teachings. From the sixteenth to the nineteenth centuries the sultanate of Brunei, which extended throughout northern Borneo, was one of the most important Islamic centres in Southeast Asia, with close links with Islamic religious authorities in the Malay peninsula and the Middle East. Many Bruneians studied in centres of Islamic learning in Arabia and performed the *hajj*. After Wahhabi teachings came to dominate Islamic education in Arabia in the 1920s, al-Azhar University in Cairo, with its then more open and moderate approach to religion, became the principal destination for, and dominant influence on, Brunei's religious scholars.[15]

From the 1980s, Darul Arqam, known in Brunei as the Jama'at Arqam, and the Tabligh movement, a fundamentalist group active in Indonesia, extended their activities to Brunei. Darul Arqam was banned in 1991, when its proselytising became too aggressive. The government maintains tight control of political and religious activities (a teacher of Islam, for instance, is required to have a licence). As a result, no Islamic party or radical Islamic movement has emerged. The Islamic revival in Brunei has instead been channelled into cultural manifestations of orthodox Islam, for instance in a greater emphasis on Islamic education, public appearance and dress.[16]

The oil boom of the 1970s and Brunei's expanding revenues in the latter part of the twentieth century allowed Bruneians to participate more actively in international exchanges and worldwide Muslim religious activities, and to undertake concrete acts of solidarity with Muslims elsewhere. Thus, the Sultan of Brunei helped to fund the arming and training of Bosnian Muslim forces in the mid-1990s. Brunei has also donated funds for humanitarian relief in Bangladesh, Kosovo and Aceh.

Islam as the unifying factor in Moro identity

Philippine Muslims are collectively known as Moros, the name given to them by the Spanish in the sixteenth century, or as Bangsamoro (literally 'the Moro nation'). Most are Sunni of the Shafi'ite school.[17] Christian Filipinos have been oriented culturally towards the West – initially towards Spain, which brought Catholicism, then later towards the US, which brought the English language, democratic political institutions and American popular culture and lifestyle. The Muslims of the southern Philippines, on the other hand, remain rooted in the Islamised Malay world.[18]

Islam had been introduced by the fourteenth century spreading throughout the Sulu archipelago and Mindanao. There are at least 13 distinct ethnolinguistic communities of Moros. The most important in Mindanao are the Maranao and the closely-related Ilanun around Lake Lanao, and the Maguindanao of Cotabato. In the Sulu archipelago, the most important groups are the Tausug on the island of Jolo (Sulu); the Yakan of Basilan island; the Samal in Tawi-Tawi and adjacent islands; and the Jama Mapun of Cagayan de Sulu. Together, they constitute approximately 17% of the population of the southern Philippines.[19]

Like other Southeast Asian Muslims, the Moros have retained many pre-Islamic beliefs and rituals. Before the Islamic resurgence of the late twentieth century, much of the knowledge about Islam among the Moros was handed down by word of mouth, and was connected with folk beliefs. There was general ignorance of the Koran, and even of the most rudimentary teachings of Islam. The *adat* or customary law was markedly different from *sharia*, and animism and animistic rituals abounded.[20]

The Muslim areas of the southern Philippines experienced an Islamic resurgence after the Second World War. This religious revival was intertwined, as in Malaysia, with ethnic nationalism. It was also influenced by the religious revival in neighbouring Muslim countries, in particular by the *dakwah* movement in Malaysia and by the return of Philippine Muslim scholars from al-Azhar university in Cairo and other centres of Islamic learning in the Middle East. With Saudi financial support, the Mindanao *ulama* began to build mosques and *madrassa*.[21] Before the Islamic resurgence there were relatively few mosques in Mindanao (only 54 were counted in 1918), and these were mostly built of wood and bamboo. By the 1970s, hundreds had been built, and of more permanent materials obviously influenced by

Middle Eastern and South Asian architectural styles.[22] The Islamic resurgence also saw changes in the dress code and status of women. The Muslim élites that had previously favoured Western-style clothes now embraced Islamic dress. Muslim women, who had always worn the traditional *malong* (a tubular woven fabric worn by both men and women) now began to wear Arab-style dress and to take on the hitherto unfamiliar practice of veiling.[23]

The Muslims of mainland Southeast Asia
Thailand
There are three distinct Muslim communities in Thailand: ethnic Malays in the south; an ethnically-mixed community in Bangkok; and Chinese Muslims in the north. The more integrated Bangkok Muslims have no difficulty in identifying themselves as Thai. The same is true of the Chinese Muslims, although in the north Muslim attitudes towards nationality remain coloured by earlier aggressive efforts to assimilate ethnic minorities. In the south, there was greater resistance to assimilation; religion became coupled with politics and fuelled an armed separatist movement.[24]

Figure 1 **Southern Thailand and Northern Malaysia**

Malay Muslims constitute approximately 80% of the population in the southern provinces of Pattani, Yala and Narithiwat. Their sense of identity as Malays is reinforced by frequent cross-border contacts with the northern Malaysian state of Kelantan. Ethnic Malays also constitute a majority in the province of Satun, although here integration has been more successful. Most Muslims in Satun now speak Thai, and the province's main communications links are northwards to central Thailand, rather than south to Malaysia.

In recent years the Bangkok government has adopted a more liberal approach towards southern Muslims, taking steps to improve their economic and social conditions, encouraging their participation at all levels in the administration, allowing teaching in the local Malay dialect and funding the construction of mosques. Islamic schools, both government- and privately-funded, are thriving throughout southern Thailand.[25]

Cambodia

When the Khmer Rouge came to power in 1975, there were 150,000 to 200,000 Muslims in Cambodia. One current estimate puts today's figure at 217,000, or 2% of the total population.[26] Most Cambodian Muslims are ethnic Malays or Cham; the majority adhere to the Shafi'ite school of Sunni Islam, though traditionalist Cham combine Islamic beliefs with ancient non-Muslim traditions and rites.[27] Radical interpretations of Islam were unknown in Cambodia until 1991, when the country emerged from a decade and a half of Khmer Rouge terror and civil war and opened up to the outside world. Since then, external funding, largely Saudi, has financed an expansion of the country's Islamic infrastructure, from about 20 mosques in 1991 to 150, another 200 places of worship and an extensive Islamic schooling system.[28] Penetration of Cambodian Muslim society by foreign elements was facilitated by the devastation of the religious establishment under the Khmer Rouge (only 20 of the 113 most prominent Cham clergy survived), and by the weakness of government institutions and services.

Burma (Myanmar)

Most sources estimate that 4% of the population of Burma (Myanmar) is Muslim.[29] Muslim leaders believe that the figure may be as high as 10%, but there has been no official census since Burma gained its independence from the British in 1948.[30] The majority of Burmese Muslims are descendants of Indian Muslims who settled in Burma under the British. Unlike other Southeast Asian Muslims, their cultural orientation is towards South Asia, rather than the Malay world. There is also a separate group of Muslims with an older history in Burma, the Rohingya, whose contact with Islam dates back to Arab traders of the eighth century. Succeeding centuries saw an influx of Arabs, Persians, Indians and Turks, who intermarried with the local inhabitants.

During the British colonial period and the early years of independence, Muslims played an important role in the administration and civil society, as well as in business and cultural activities. From the early 1960s, successive military regimes have sought to strengthen their support by identifying with Theravada Buddhism, the majority religion, and have sanctioned varying degrees of discrimination against Muslims.[31] Much of the current concern about possible Islamic radicalism in Burma centres on Rohingya organisations based along the country's border with Bangladesh.[32]

Shi'ism in Southeast Asia

Shi'ism, though very much a minority stream in Southeast Asian Islam, has gained in popularity since the Iranian revolution, particularly among the young. In Indonesia, Shi'ite institutions devoted to educational and missionary work have developed in Java, Sumatra and Kalimantan, and are active in Jakarta. The most prominent are the Mutahari and Jawad foundations in Bandung, West Sumatra, and the Muntadzar Foundation in Jakarta. The Pesantren al-Hadi in Pekalongan in Central Java has adopted the educational system of Qom in Iran, and all teachers are graduates of Qom schools.[33]

Iran is trying to gain a foothold in Southeast Asia by working with local Shi'ite groups. The Iranian organisation Union of the Ahal al-Beit Youth Fund (IPABI) has a branch in Indonesia. Iran also operates through Hizbollah, which maintains close links with the Pan-Malay Islamic Party (PAS) and recruits young Southeast Asian Muslims to study in the Middle East. According to sources in the region, Hizbollah is active in Thailand and operates through the Iranian Embassy in Manila.

Conclusion

Islam in Southeast Asia is complex and dynamic. The majority of Muslims in the region are embedded in the Malay world, which provides the cultural, social and political context for Southeast Asian conceptions of Islam. This context accounts for the marked differences in the political expression of Islam between Southeast Asia and the Middle East. At the same time, Southeast Asia's Muslim communities have for centuries been susceptible to outside influences, and are increasingly exposed to the broader religious and political movements in the Muslim world, including those that convey extremist and radical messages. The following chapters analyse the impact of external and domestic forces in the evolution of political Islam in the major Southeast Asian countries.

Chapter 2

Indonesia: the Jihad project

The relationship between Islam and the state has been one of the key unresolved questions in the political development of Muslim-majority Southeast Asian countries since their independence. In Indonesia, disagreements between advocates of an Islamic state and those who wanted to establish the new republic on a non-confessional basis were resolved in favour of the latter. The 1945 Constitution enshrined Pancasila – which defined the national identity without reference to Islam – as the national ideology.[1] The only concessions made to Islam were the retention of colonial-era Islamic courts with jurisdiction over family law, mainly marriage and divorce. Muslim dissatisfaction with the secular orientation of the republic, and disagreements over the role of Muslim militias in the new national army, led to the Darul Islam rebellion in West Java in 1948. The revolt spread to South Sulawesi and Aceh, and was not fully extinguished until the 1960s. Darul Islam significantly influenced the ideological development of some of the most virulent strains of current Indonesian Islamic extremism.[2]

During Indonesia's period of parliamentary government in the 1950s, Muslim interests were represented by two major political parties, Nahdlatul Ulama and Masjumi, a coalition of modernist Muslim political groups. Masjumi was banned in 1960, when President Sukarno embarked on the authoritarian 'guided democracy' phase of his rule. This was also the heyday of the powerful Indonesian Communist Party (PKI). Secular anti-communists made common cause with Muslims against the greater threat of communism, and Muslim militants were encouraged to play a role in the destruction of the PKI.

Islam under the new order

Under Suharto's New Order regime (1967–98), political Islam was tamed and Pancasila was made the sole ideological basis for all social and political organisations. The only vehicle allowed for the representation of Muslim interests was the United Development Party (Partai Persatuan Pembangunan – PPP), an officially-recognised and controlled party with Pancasila, not Islam, as its sole ideology.[3] For most of the New Order, the government labelled political Islam as the 'extreme right', ranking just below the communists, the 'extreme left', in the hierarchy of political threats.

The seeds of today's Islamic upsurge in Indonesia were sown in the later years of the New Order, when Suharto, having lost support within the military, sought to cultivate Muslims as a countervailing force. His most visible step in this direction was a highly publicised *hajj* in June 1991. Through one of his charitable foundations, Suharto also supported the construction and maintenance of thousands of mosques and *madrassa*. The government passed legislation establishing the equality of Islamic courts with other types, and returning to them jurisdiction over inheritance disputes.[4]

Suharto courted the 'neo-modernist' Muslims represented by the Dewan Dakwah Islamiyah Indonesia (DDII – Indonesian Islamic Propagation Council), an organisation with a strict Salafi orientation that had previously been a strong critic of the regime. The reconciliation was facilitated by the close relations between younger DDII leaders and some of Suharto's 'green' (Islamic) generals, who rose to leading positions in the military in the mid-1990s.[5] Suharto's son-in-law, Major-General (later Lieutenant-General) Prabowo Subianto, was instrumental in building a support base among Muslim clerics, called the Committee of Solidarity with the Muslim World (KISDI).[6] KISDI and the DDII were later to play an important role in supporting Laskar Jihad and other militant groups.

A milestone in the Islamisation process was the establishment of the Ikatan Cendekiawan Muslim Se-Indonesia (ICMI – Association of Indonesian Muslim Intellectuals), chaired by the Minister for Research and Technology and later president B. J. Habibie, with strong support from Suharto. ICMI was key in establishing new Islamic institutions, such as the Indonesian Islamic Bank, the *Republika* daily newspaper and the Centre for Information and Development Studies (CIDES). It also mobilised Muslim intellectuals and laid the ideological and political foundations of the post-Suharto upsurge of political Islam.[7]

Islam and post-new order politics

Suharto's downfall in 1998 unleashed political forces that the New Order had suppressed or controlled. The new political environment enabled Muslim extremists to launch what Michael Davis calls the 'jihad project', an attempt to undermine the country's pluralist political institutions and establish an Islamic state.[8] At the same time, however, mainstream Indonesian Islam remained firmly anchored in the framework of Pancasila. Both the traditionalist Nahdlatul Ulama and the modernist Muhammadiyah resisted (and continue to resist) efforts to redefine the state in Islamic terms.[9] There are, however, extremists within the mainstream Muslim organisations. Muhammadiyah's Deputy Chairman Din Syamsuddin represents one such faction. Syamsuddin, who is also the Secretary-General of the Indonesian Ulama Council, is a former functionary in Golkar, the governing party under Suharto, and had been associated with the Islamic tilt of Suharto's latter years. Syamsuddin questioned Osama bin Laden's responsibility for the attacks in New York and Washington in September 2001 and, after the arrest of suspected terrorists in Malaysia and Singapore in December 2001, warned the Indonesian security forces against similar action.[10]

Parliamentary elections in June 1999, the first genuinely free polls since the 1950s, exposed the lack of popular support for explicitly Islamic parties. Two secular parties, Megawati Sukarnoputri's Indonesian Democratic Party-Struggle (Partai Demokrasi Indonesia-Perjuangan – PDI-P) and Golkar, together received 57% of the vote. Two 'inclusive' Muslim parties (that is, open to non-Muslims), Wahid's National Awakening Party (Partai Kebangkitan Bangsa – PKB) and the Muhammadiyah-linked National Mandate Party (Partai Amanat Nasional – PAN), won 12% and 8% respectively, and the PPP, the 'official' Islamic party under Suharto, received 11%. Militant Islamic parties received less than 6%.[11]

The Islamist camp comprises two relatively small parties, the Crescent and Star Party (Partai Bulan Bintang – PBB) and the Justice Party (Partai Keadilan). Although ideologically congruent, the two have very different social bases. The Crescent and Star Party is grounded in rural communities in Sumatra and Kalimantan; its constituency is older and less educated than the Justice Party's, and has its roots in earlier Muslim political tradition.[12] The more dynamic Justice Party originated in Islamic study circles at Indonesian universities, particularly the University of Indonesia and the Bandung Institute of Technology, and its leaders have been educated in Indonesia and the West. It considers itself a 'cadre', not a mass party. Its goal is not short-term electoral gain, but to propagate a correct interpretation of Islam as a way of life and politics. Despite its Islamist ideology, the party seeks to project a moderate and reasonable public image, and claims to seek change through peaceful means.[13]

Laskar Jihad and the religious war in Eastern Indonesia

Although militant Islamic parties captured only a small percentage of the vote in the 1999 elections, radical organisations in Java have used religious violence elsewhere in Indonesia to mobilise supporters and to attack the central government. Laskar Jihad, the militia of the Ahlul Sunnah Wal Jamaah Communication Forum, is the best known of these groups.

Laskar Jihad was founded by Ja'afar Umar Thalib, an Indonesian of Yemeni descent who pursued Islamic studies in the Mawdudi Institute in Pakistan and took part in the war in Afghanistan in the late 1980s. The organisation adheres to the Wahhabi school, and recruits its members from among the poorer and less-educated segments of the population, especially the young urban poor. As with other jihadist organisations, the group claims as its mission social work and Muslim education, but its primary business and *raison d'être* was the *jihad* in Maluku in eastern Indonesia.

Violence between Christians and Muslims in Maluku broke out in 1999. The causes are complex, to do with regional as well as ethnic and religious tensions. The inhabitants of the outer islands – Sumatra, Sulawesi and Maluku – have long resented and resisted Javanese domination. That resentment was exacerbated by the Suharto government's policy of transmigration, whereby people from heavily-populated Java were transferred to the outer islands. Relations between Maluku's Christian and Muslim communities had been friendly and cooperative. In Halmahera, for instance, they helped each other to build places of worship.[14] However, the arrival

Figure 2 Areas of conflict in Indonesia

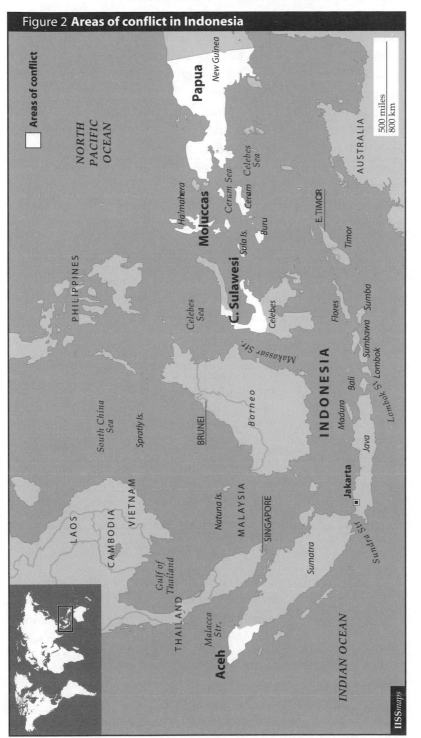

of migrants, mostly Muslims, from other regions upset established social and economic arrangements and altered the demographic balance. This, together with local political rivalries and the suspected involvement of elements of the military associated with the Suharto regime, contributed to the conflict.[15]

In early 2000, Laskar Jihad dispatched hundreds of armed volunteers to Ambon, the political and economic hub of Maluku. From their training camp at Bogor in West Java, where they were said to have received training by members of the army's Kopassus special forces, they travelled to Surabaya, and embarked for Ambon unhindered. The government's military forces in Maluku were too few and too thinly stretched to control the violence; anecdotal evidence suggests that, as the sectarian conflict intensified, discipline collapsed.[16] Other Muslim irregulars also operated in Maluku alongside the Laskar Jihad. These included the Laskar Mujahidin, a group associated with Abu Bakar Bashir's network. Laskar Mujahidin's preference was for hit-and-run attacks, with the aim of destroying churches or killing priests or other Christian leaders, rather than to secure ground, as Laskar Jihad was attempting to do. The two groups did not cooperate and sometimes clashed.[17]

The authorities did not regain control until 2001, when an élite battalion was dispatched to Ambon to restore order. This unit, known as the Yon Gab or joint battalion, took aggressive action against Laskar Jihad, including a June 2001 raid that left 23 people dead. These tactics were criticised by Muslim politicians, who claimed that the unit was anti-Muslim and demanded its recall. Protests by Laskar Jihad supporters, including mainstream Muslim politicians, caused the central government to withdraw the combined battalion in November 2001, and replace it with a Kopassus (Army Special Forces) unit.[18]

Communal conflict also flared up in Sulawesi, where large-scale violence between Muslims and Christians broke out in April 2000 in Poso, a region roughly evenly divided between the two communities. Hundreds were killed. In August, the governors of Sulawesi's five provinces declared a truce, but violence broke out again in April 2001 after a local court condemned to death three Christian commanders accused of involvement in the previous year's disturbances. Christians considered the sentence biased given that no Muslims stood trial.[19] The following August, Laskar Jihad declared a *jihad* in Poso and began to dispatch hundreds of fighters to the district, where Laskar Mujahidin and another extremist militia, Laskar Jundullah, were already active. The arrival of Laskar Jihad forces decisively tilted the balance against the Christians. The situation stabilised in December 2001, when the national government sent two battalions of soldiers and police (composed predominantly of Christians from North Sulawesi) to the Christian areas. Other troops took over checkpoints previously manned by Muslim militants.

The government's approach was to separate the combatants, while avoiding being seen as taking sides, and to try to mediate an agreement between the two camps. This yielded results in the so-called Malino I and II agreements (after the town in South Sulawesi where they were negotiated), in which Muslim and Christian representatives undertook to end the hostilities in Poso and Maluku respectively and disarm their respective militias. Laskar Jihad denounced the agreements, and in April 2002 instigated an attack on the Christian village of Soya near Ambon, a serious challenge to the Malino II agreement and one of the factors behind the arrest of the group's leader, Jaafar Thalib, in May 2002.[20]

Laskar Jihad's hostility to the Malino agreements reflected its dependence on conflict and violence to justify its existence. Its tactics, such as targeting civilians, are part of a sustained effort to polarise the Muslim and Christian communities. This not only advances Laskar Jihad's goals in Maluku, but also increases tensions and religious polarisation in other parts of Indonesia, thereby promoting the group's larger objectives.[21]

Despite their limited grassroots support, Indonesia's Islamic radicals are adept at using modern mass communications and are capable of influencing public opinion.[22] Laskar Jihad has succeeded in presenting itself as the defender of beleaguered Muslims in eastern Indonesia, a view accepted even by some moderates. Even critics of Laskar Jihad's goals and tactics note that the group defended Muslims in Maluku when the government was unable or unwilling to do so. The perception of Laskar Jihad as a defender of Muslim interests enabled it to push mainstream politicians into supporting its positions. At the mass rally in Jakarta in January 2000 that launched the campaign for a *jihad* in Maluku, speakers included Amien Rais, the Speaker of the People's Consultative Assembly (MPR), and the current Vice-President, Hamzah Haz.

Indonesia and the war on terrorism

Indonesia has many characteristics that could make it a hospitable environment for terrorists and extremist groups: long and porous borders, weak and dysfunctional government and law-enforcement institutions and radical Islamic networks. However, until the bomb attack in Bali on 12 October 2002 political weakness meant that the government found it difficult to take meaningful action.

In October 1999, the People's Consultative Assembly (MPR) unexpectedly elected Abdurrahman Wahid, a nearly blind Muslim cleric in frail health, as the country's president. Wahid, better known as Gus ('Elder Brother') Dur, headed the Nahdlatul Ulama. As vice-president, the MPR elected Megawati Sukarnoputri, the daughter of Indonesia's founding President Sukarno. Although Wahid's party, the PKB, garnered only 12% of the vote, the other Muslim parties backed him to block the election of Megawati, the leader of the largest single parliamentary bloc. However, Wahid's erratic style of governance and his alienation of members of the coalition that brought him to power led to his removal by the MPR in July 2001, and Megawati's accession to the presidency.

As a secular political leader, Megawati's Islamic credentials are weak; in the run-up to the 1999 elections, A. M. Saefuddin, a member of Habibie's cabinet, asserted that she was not a Muslim, but a Hindu. Saefuddin pointed to Megawati's frequent appearances at Hindu temples in Bali, and asked whether Indonesians would accept a Hindu as president.[23] Moreover, her government depends on Muslim parties for its parliamentary majority; these are the same parties that came together to block her accession to the presidency in 1999. Hamzah Haz, leader of the PPP, the largest Muslim political party, only dropped his opposition in 2001, when he was elected to the vice-presidency as a Muslim counterweight to Megawati. Haz opposed US operations in Afghanistan and, just days after 11 September, told worshippers at a Jakarta mosque that the attacks would 'cleanse the sins of the United States', a statement that infuriated US officials and embarrassed the president.

Megawati and her advisers saw great risks and few advantages in moving against the radicals, even if this meant frustrating the US and some of Indonesia's neighbours. Indonesian officials explained the government's caution by noting that, unlike Malaysia and Singapore, Indonesia lacked the equivalent of an

Internal Security Act that would allow the authorities greater latitude in dealing with suspected terrorists. The authorities could not move against suspects without sufficient evidence to persuade not only a court, but also Muslim public opinion. Officials also argued that the political and ethnic environment in Indonesia, a country almost 90% Muslim, was different from Singapore's (a multi-ethnic state), the Philippines' (predominantly Christian) or Malaysia's (majority Muslim, but with a strong government).[24]

Nevertheless, the government began to show signs of greater resolve. In May 2002, Laskar Jihad leader Ja'afar was arrested and charged with inciting religious violence. Despite protests from Muslim political parties and radical Islamic organisations such as KISDI and demonstrations in Jakarta, the arrest exposed the weakness of the radicals' position and Megawati faced no major political repercussions.[25] Ja'afar continued to enjoy the support of some sectors of Muslim public opinion and the indulgence of mainstream Muslim politicians who sympathised with his goals or hoped to derive some political advantage from their association. Nevertheless, by late 2002 Laskar Jihad's influence was clearly in decline as international pressure on the government to crack down on extremists increased, and some of the military and political factions that had helped the organisation in its ascendancy came to see it as more of a liability than an asset. Three days after the Bali attack, Laskar Jihad announced that it had closed its headquarters and disbanded, though it is more likely that the group has decided to lower its profile until conditions become more favourable.

Another sign of the government's more robust position came in summer 2002, with the arrest and transfer to US custody of Omar al-Faruq, identified as the most senior al-Qaeda operative in Southeast Asia. US and Indonesian intelligence agencies picked up al-Faruq's trail when his mobile-phone number was found programmed into the phones of two captured operatives, Abu Zubaidah, al-Qaeda's chief of operations, and the Indonesian extremist Agus Dwikarna. Al-Faruq's reported confessions, which included allegations of two assassination plots against Megawati, were widely reported in the international media. According to al-Faruq, al-Qaeda had encouraged the efforts of Abu Bakar Bashir, the suspected ideological leader of Jemaah Islamiyah, to spark a religious war in Indonesia and implement his vision of an Islamic state. Bomb attacks against churches in December 2000, in which 18 people were killed and over 100 injured, were said to have been carried out with Bashir's knowledge, approval and logistical support. Al-Faruq also revealed plots to launch a suicide mission against a US Navy ship, similar to the attack on the *USS Cole*, and to bomb US embassies in the region.[26]

Information from al-Faruq led to the arrest of Seyam Reda, a German national of Syrian descent who claimed to be a correspondent for the Arab television network al-Jazeera. A search of Reda's home produced videotapes showing arms distribution and weapons training in an area of conflict in Indonesia. The Indonesian authorities were initially uncertain about Reda's role, though it appears that German and Indonesian intelligence agencies now believe that he was head of finance for al-Qaeda in Southeast Asia.[27] According to a well-placed Jakarta correspondent, funds were channelled to Reda, described as the 'paymaster' of a terrorist ring in Indonesia, through the Saudi-based al-Haramain foundation.[28]

The Bali bombing and its aftermath

Indonesia's moment of truth in the war on terrorism came on 12 October 2002 with the bomb attacks in Kuta on the island of Bali, the worst terrorist incident in the country's history. The bombings left 202 people dead and over 300 wounded, most of them Australians and other foreign tourists. The most damaging of the three bomb attacks on Bali, carried out by two separate teams, was the car bomb explosion that destroyed the Sari Club in Kuta's entertainment district. Another bomb was carried into a bar, Paddy's Club, by a suicide bomber named Iqbal, a close friend of Imam Samudra, an Indonesian later identified as the chief organiser of the attack. This was the first suicide bomb attack in modern Indonesian history. The third bomb, at the US Consular Agency, caused no casualties.[29]

Defence Minister Matori Abdul Djalil and other Indonesian officials who had hitherto questioned the presence of al-Qaeda cells in Indonesia now asserted that the bombing had been carried out by al-Qaeda with the support of local collaborators. According to senior Indonesian intelligence sources, a Yemeni al-Qaeda operative named Syahfullah and a Malaysian named Zubair had played key roles in the Bali bombing. Zubair was believed to have been responsible for the surveillance and mapping of the target sites before the attack. Syahfullah is believed to have coordinated the attack with Imam

Samudra and Ali Gufron (alias Mukhlas), a senior operative in Jemaah Islamiyah. Both Samudra and Mukhlas were later arrested by the Indonesian authorities.[30]

For the government, the immediate challenge was to find a way to respond without seeming to give in to outside pressure. On 19 October, a week after the attack, Megawati signed two emergency anti-terrorism decrees. One provided general guidelines, while the other was designed to deal specifically with the Bali incident. The measures, which were endorsed by the leaders of Nahdlatul Ulama and Muhammadiyah, empowered the authorities to arrest suspected terrorists based on intelligence information and to hold them for up to a week without charge, or longer if the intelligence justified doing so.[31] The investigation into the attacks developed rapidly in the following weeks. The identification of the chassis of the vehicle used in the bombing of the Sari Club led to the arrest of the owner, a motorcycle mechanic named Amrozi, which in turn led to the arrests of Imam Samudra, Amrozi's brother Mukhlas and other suspects.[32]

Meanwhile, after hesitating for over a week, the authorities arrested Bashir in Solo, though in connection with the church bombings in December 2000 and not the Bali attack.[33] The police also arrested Muhammad Habib Rizieq, the leader of the Islam Defenders' Front (FPI), an extortion group in Islamic guise known for raiding bars and nightclubs in Jakarta. Bashir's arrest was criticised by some Muslim leaders, who alleged that the government was bowing to foreign pressure.[34] However, leading Muslim moderates supported the move. Bashir also lost the support of the previously sympathetic Hamzah Haz, who stated that his arrest was based on the law and not on international pressure.[35]

The question of whether Bashir was responsibile for the Bali attacks remains controversial. According to a December 2002 report by the International Crisis Group (ICG), he is said to have opposed the bombing for tactical reasons, but the more radical faction of the Jemaah Islamiyah prevailed. The ICG concluded that Bashir is unlikely to have been the mastermind behind the attack.[36] Nevertheless, the investigation has been moving closer to Bashir and to the core of Jemaah Islamiyah.

The Indonesian military and Islam

An important variable in the development of political Islam in

Indonesia is the relationship between Islam and the military. Indonesian military culture places great value on the unity and cohesion of the military institution and on the country's pluralist principles. The curriculum at all levels of the military education system emphasises indoctrination in the national philosophy, Pancasila. By and large, the Indonesian military has distrusted political Islam, partly because of its experience in suppressing Muslim rebellions in the 1950s and 1960s – which accustomed the armed forces to viewing radical Islam as a threat to the stability of the state – and partly because the military leadership has been largely dominated by secular nationalists.

Whatever its shortcomings, the military is broadly representative of the country's diverse population, though Christians are present in a larger proportion than in the population at large and have reached high levels in the hierarchy. General Benny Moerdani, a Christian, enjoyed significant power during his tenure as armed forces commander and Minister of Defence in the 1980s and early 1990s, but no Christian general has risen to similar rank since. When Moerdani fell from power in 1993, the 'green' faction, under new armed forces commander General Feisal Tanjung and the army chief of staff, General Hartono, gained the ascendancy. Officers with an Islamic orientation replaced Christians or *abangan* (syncretic) Muslims in key positions. This phase in the evolution of the military coincided with Suharto's opening to the Muslim political sectors.

In the last year of his rule, Suharto tried to restore the balance between 'green' and *merah putih* ('red and white' or secularist-nationalist) officers with the appointment of General Wiranto, a middle-of-the-road officer, as armed forces commander. Nevertheless, 'green' generals and their Muslim political backers retained considerable influence. This was well demonstrated with the appointment of a Christian, Lieutenant-General Johny Lumintang, to head the Strategic Reserve (Kostrad) during the Habibie administration. Despite his impeccable professional credentials, the move generated such intense Muslim opposition that he was replaced before he had served a day in the post.

During the immediate post-Suharto period, some military sectors were believed to have supported, or turned a blind eye to, the activities of radical Muslim groups.[37] Laskar Jihad was reportedly supported and financed by elements of the military.[38] The deployment of Laskar Jihad fighters from Java to Ambon in 2000, against President Wahid's explicit orders, would not have been possible without the acquiescence or support of some military authorities. As the political situation became more stable under Megawati, the value of these relationships diminished. By early 2003, the military appeared to have resumed its role as a barrier against religious extremism, and the prospects for non-Muslim officers appeared to have improved. The division of the officer corps between 'green' and 'red and white' camps, notable during the 1990s, seemed to have eased.[39]

Conclusion

At least until the Bali bombing, Indonesia was the weak link in the war on terrorism in Southeast Asia. Diminished state capacity, political and economic vulnerability and the unresolved issue of the role of Islam in politics made Indonesia an attractive target for Islamic extremists – both tactically, as a base for recruitment and a launch pad for attacks, and strategically, as a potential component of their vision of an Islamic state in Southeast Asia. In the first years of Indonesia's new democracy, militant Islamic factions were able to exert greater influence than their numbers would seem to warrant. One reason for this was the lack of a countervailing mobilisation by Muslim moderates, which allowed radicals to exploit Islam for their own political purposes. Another was complacency within the government.

The Bali bombing changed the political environment, prompting a crackdown on extremists and a greater willingness by secular politicians and moderate Muslims to challenge the radicals. The qualified support of the major Muslim organisations for a stronger anti-terrorist stance, and the vice-president's distancing of himself from Bashir, suggest that the Megawati government enjoys more latitude in responding to religious extremists. However, whether this new-found resolve will be sustained, and whether the shift in the wider public mood will fundamentally alter the pattern of political competition in Indonesia, remains an open question.

Chapter 3

Islamic militancy in Malaysia and Singapore

Malaysia: the slippery slope towards an Islamic state

In Malaysia, political Islam has taken on characteristics quite different from those of its counterpart in Indonesia. Whereas in Indonesia national identity has been defined in non-religious terms, Malaysia defines itself as an Islamic country. The political debate within the dominant Malay community is therefore not whether Malaysia should be a secular or an Islamic state, but what kind of Islamic state it should be.

Islamisation and political competition

This question is the crux of the competition between UMNO, the dominant partner in the ruling Barisan Nasional (National Front), and the Islamic fundamentalist opposition party (Partai Islam Se-Malaysia – PAS).

PAS was established as the Pan Malaysian Islamic Party (PMIP) in 1951 by dissidents from UMNO's Bureau of Religious Affairs, and it has participated in every parliamentary election in Malaysia since 1955. In 1959, it came to power in the states of Kelantan and Terengganu; in Kelantan, it has subsequently kept control, with the exception of 1978–1990; it lost control of Terengganu in 1961, but regained it in 1999. From 1973 to 1978, the party formed part of the National Front, until forced out after the UMNO-inspired overthrow of the PAS-controlled government of Kelantan. From the outset, the party's goal was a *sharia*-based state in which economic, political and social systems conformed thoroughly to Islamic values, but during the first three decades of its existence its ideology also had a strong tinge of Malay nationalism.

After parliamentary elections in 1978, in which PAS suffered one of its worst defeats, the party began to take a decidedly more theocratic cast. Its reorientation as a more religious party was the result of several factors. The *ulama* began to play a more important role in party affairs, particularly in Kelantan. There was also an infusion of cadres and ideology from the Islamic Youth Movement (Angkatan Belia Islam Malaysia – ABIM), which contributed a new ideological thrust and orientation. ABIM, a university-based non-governmental organisation headed by future Deputy Prime Minister Anwar Ibrahim from 1974–1982, laid the ideological foundations of modern political Islam in Malaysia. It organised training programmes for its members and ran schools throughout the country. Its primary aim was to inculcate what it considered to be a proper understanding of Islam in the population, particularly young Muslims. The group criticised the government for promoting Malay nationalism on the grounds that this subordinated Islamic identity to a narrow ethnic concept. Like other Islamist movements, ABIM also criticised economic inequality, Western-oriented economic development models and cultural influence, corruption and the abuse of internal-security laws.[1]

A turning-point in Malaysia's political evolution came in 1982, when a new generation, many with an ABIM background, took over the leadership of PAS.[2] The party came under the ideological influence of the Iranian revolution, accepting the Iranian concept of the supremacy of the religious hierarchy. PAS began to propose a vision of the Islamic state that included an elected parliament with limited legislative authority, subordinated to a religious body, the Council of Ulama, and with *sharia* as the exclusive source of law.[3] PAS also began to characterise itself and its followers as *mustazaffin* (the oppressed) as against *mustakbirin* (the oppressors), a terminology popularised by the Iranian revolution.[4]

While ABIM was providing much of PAS' new leadership, in 1982 the leading ABIM personality, Anwar Ibrahim, and a number of his followers joined UMNO, which had launched its own Islamisation programme under new Prime Minister Mahathir bin Mohamad. This was known as the Penerapan Nilai-nilai Islam (Inculcation of Islamic Values). UMNO strategy since 1982 has been to accommodate Islam through pro-Islamic rhetoric and initiatives such as the Dakwah Foundation, to coordinate Islamic propagation activities throughout the country; the International Islamic University; compulsory 'Islamic civilisation' courses for Muslim university students; and Islamic banking and insurance schemes.[5] The strategy has been to blunt PAS' appeal by blurring the distinctions between the two parties' agendas.

In response to PAS' demand for an Islamic state, UMNO leaders took the position that Malaysia was already an Islamic country (even a 'fundamentalist' Islamic country by virtue of its subscription to the 'fundamental principles' of Islam).[6] This manifests itself in diverse ways, including the offering of Muslim prayers at official functions, the construction of mosques by the state, the holding of Koran-reading competitions, and state agencies' organisation of the *hajj*. Nevertheless, the Mahathir government's Islamisation campaign has not changed the fundamental structure of the country's legal, political and administrative system, which is based on the British model and to a large extent reflects the Western political tradition.

Splits within UMNO

The prospects for political Islam in Malaysia were dealt a significant blow in the late 1990s with the dismissal of Anwar, the Deputy Prime Minister and Mahathir's heir apparent. The rift between the two surfaced in differences over how to handle the effects of the economic crisis of 1997–98. Anwar, who was also finance minister, favoured stabilisation and demanded that the government halt the bailout of indebted companies, stop funding large public projects and clean up the banking system. Mahathir rejected this advice and decided instead on a course of strict currency and capital controls.[7] Against the background of political change in Indonesia, Anwar presented himself as the avatar of reform, and his admirers dismissed Mahathir as an obsolete authoritarian destined to share Suharto's fate.

Underestimating Mahathir turned out to be a fatal political mistake. The prime minister preempted a challenge by Anwar for the UMNO leadership by tightening the rules for the nomination of leadership candidates and removing officials loyal to Anwar.[8] On 2 September 1998 Mahathir dismissed his former deputy, calling him morally unfit. Anwar was arrested 18 days later. He was convicted in April 1999 on four charges of corruption, and sentenced to six years in prison. A second trial, on charges of sodomy with his former driver, opened in June 1999 and closed the following year with Anwar's conviction, and his sentencing to a further nine years in jail. Anwar was also disqualified from holding public office for five years after his release.

Anwar's contention that he was the victim of a conspiracy resonated with the public. In elections in November 1999, PAS made significant inroads into traditional UMNO strongholds. It increased its parliamentary representation from seven to 27 seats, regained control of Terengganu state and became the main opposition party. The UMNO-led National Front coalition retained its two-thirds majority in parliament, but suffered substantial losses in the Malay belt of northern states. Its share of the vote fell to 56%, and the number of parliamentary seats it held dropped from 94 to 72 (in peninsular Malaysia, UMNO's strength went down from 78 to 60, out of 144 seats). For the first time, UMNO had fewer seats in parliament than its coalition partners combined.[9]

Despite these electoral losses, Anwar's downfall was a major setback for political Islam in Malaysia. As Singaporean political scientist Hussin Mutalib noted several years before, Anwar had long been known for his preference for the 'Islamic alternative', and had been instrumental in establishing and developing Islamic policies and institutions. Had he succeeded Mahathir, he would have found himself under great pressure from some of his followers to move Malaysia closer to conformity with Islamic principles.[10] His removal from Malaysian politics has precluded this possibility.

Islamists in retreat

As elsewhere in Southeast Asia, 11 September and the war on terrorism significantly altered the Malaysian political environment, provoking a flow of moderate Muslims and non-Muslims back to the ruling coalition. In response, PAS abandoned the moderate posture that it had assumed for the 1999 elections and radicalised its rhetoric. It declared a figurative *jihad* against the US, and mounted demonstrations in front of the US Embassy. PAS also attempted to exploit the Palestinian issue (where it shares common ground with moderate Muslims) by sponsoring a forum with Hamas and Hizbollah militants.[11] This radical posture was, however, a serious tactical error as it frightened and alienated moderate Muslims, and PAS' non-Muslim political allies. The ethnic Chinese opposition Democratic Action Party (DAP) broke off its alliance. The Partai Keadilan, which represented Anwar's supporters, also lost credibility because of its association with the radicalised PAS.

The government took full advantage of these missteps to break the opposition's momentum and put PAS on the defensive. In August 2001, the authorities detained Nik Adli Nik Aziz, the son of Nik Abdul Aziz Nik Mat, PAS' spiritual leader and chief minister of Kelantan state, and other activists, and suggested that PAS had been infiltrated by terrorists. Nik Adli headed a clandestine group known as the Kumpulan Militan Malaysia (Malaysian Militant Group), sometimes called Kumpulan Mujahidin Malaysia (Malaysian Mujahidin Group) or KMM, which was implicated in terrorist attacks in Malaysia and has been linked to regional terrorist groups (see Chapter 5). Although PAS denied any links to terrorists, the UMNO-led National Front registered major successes in three by-elections after 11 September, and Malaysian political analysts expected it to reverse PAS gains in parliamentary polls to be held by November 2004.

PAS leaders appear to have taken these setbacks philosophically. They understand that, in Malaysia's multi-ethnic and multi-religious society, their political programme can only be implemented incrementally. They say that the two PAS-controlled states, Kelantan and Terengganu, are, testing grounds for the party's programme.[12] However, there are limits to what PAS can achieve at state level. The PAS-controlled legislature in Kelantan passed a law in 1993 to implement Islamic criminal law in the state, but could not enforce it without amending the federal constitution, which requires a two-thirds vote in parliament. This is not likely to occur soon. The current demographic and electoral map of Malaysia rules out a PAS victory for the foreseeable future. Even if PAS were to win every parliamentary seat in the northern belt of Malay states, it would still fall well short of a majority. The two eastern states, Sarawak and Sabah, where PAS has very little strength, would remain barriers to a PAS government, as presumably would the ethnic Chinese and Indian communities that together comprise more than 30% of the electorate. PAS strategy has to take the long view. In this, it resembles other Islamist parties both within and outside Southeast Asia.

In the wake of his surprise announcement in July 2002 that he would be retiring the following year, Mahathir proposed a series of measures designed to break the hold of militant Islam on Malaysian education. Mahathir's plan includes relocating religious education in the state system to after-school classes purged of political content, close government regulation of private Islamic schools (which senior government officials believe are a breeding ground for militant Islam), and establishing compulsory national service for youths in order to break down ethnic barriers and strengthen commitment to national unity.[13] Government and business leaders are also concerned that the emphasis on religious education and the use of Malay (rather than English) as the language of instruction are making Malays less competitive in the global economy and widening the economic gap between Malays and non-Malays. The government's proposed refurbishing of education therefore serves both political and economic needs. The reforms, which would reverse longstanding UMNO policies, are controversial even within the ruling party, and will require the kind of strong leadership that might be easier for an outgoing prime minister than for an incoming government.

Singapore: Islamic militancy in a multi-ethnic city-state

The religio-political situation in Singapore is the reverse of that in Malaysia. While in Malaysia Muslim Malays are a politically dominant majority in a multi-ethnic but officially 'Islamic' state, in Singapore Muslims are a minority within an officially multi-ethnic state in which ethnic Chinese predominate. The approaches of the two governments to the management of ethno-religious relations are also different. In Malaysia, UMNO-controlled governments have pursued an ethnically and religiously conscious policy. In Singapore, the authorities have sought to blur ethnic and religious distinctions and encourage the development of a national identity independent of ethnicity and religion. Singapore's founding prime minister, Lee Kuan Yew, explicitly rejected state discrimination in favour of the ethnic Chinese. The administration has made efforts to remove the impediments and disabilities that in the past relegated the local Malays to the bottom rungs of the socio-economic scale. As a result, over the past two decades there have been significant improvements in the educational level, income and standard of living of Singapore's Malays.[14]

Nevertheless, Singapore has not been immune to the upsurge in Islamic militancy. In January and February 2002, three girls were suspended from school for wearing Muslim female headdress in contravention of school regulations. The girls' families, supported by a sector of the Singaporean Muslim community, argued that modesty and their concept of morality required the girls to wear the headdress.[15] The authorities saw the controversy as an effort to embarrass the government and to manipulate Islam for political purposes. This view was reinforced when Malaysia's PAS took sides with Muslim families, an intrusion into Singapore's internal affairs that greatly upset the authorities. More seriously from the government's perspective, the episode represented the incipient stage of a threat to the country's valued national cohesion.

The discovery in December 2001 of a terrorist cell in Singapore also illustrated the limits of economic and social policies in preventing militancy. All but one of the 13 suspects were Singaporean citizens. All had attended schools in Singapore, and six had completed military service. Most were businessmen, professionals or technical personnel. One was an aerospace technician who had taken photographs of the Paya Labar air base and the US Air Force aircraft deployed there as a potential target for attack.[16] These were not economically deprived individuals without a stake in Singaporean society. They were, on the contrary, the product of successful economic and social policies.

The implications of two decades of Islamisation in Malaysia and Indonesia also trouble Singapore. Moderate Islamic leaders in the region, Singaporean security analysts believe, are being replaced by a new, more radical generation. The Singaporeans note the Malaysian government's concern about the widening appeal of militant ideology among members of the middle class and the intelligentsia, and growing radical Islamic activism in the universities. In Indonesia, Singaporeans fear that politicians are using Islam to better position themselves with Muslims for the 2004 presidential elections; they are, however, confident that Megawati and the country's secular forces will prevail.

Conclusion

As Malaysia approaches the end of the Mahathir era, the governing coalition appears solid and likely to improve its parliamentary position in the 2004 elections. PAS is isolated, and proposed measures to restructure religious education could, if successful, reduce one of its principal sources of future strength. At the same time, the new education initiatives point to the exhaustion of the policy of Islamisation that has informed UMNO's philosophy of governance since the early 1980s. UMNO's success in finding a new balance between the expectations of its Malay constituency and the requirements of governing a modernising, multi-ethnic society will determine whether PAS' brand of political Islam will be contained as the political project of a minority within the Malay Muslim community, or whether it comes to threaten Malaysia's model of political compromise and coexistence among the country's various communities.

Malaysia's future direction is, of course, of great concern to Singapore. As a small, multi-ethnic, but predominantly ethnic Chinese island surrounded by Muslim states, and dependent on international links for its economic survival, Singapore is extremely sensitive to changes in its security environment. For this reason, the authorities are concerned not only about relations among the ethnic communities in Singapore itself, but also about the inroads of militant Islam in its larger neighbours. Singapore's success as a state rests ultimately on its ability to maintain and strengthen its national cohesion and the multi-ethnic character of its society. Beyond that, it seeks to maintain a stable order in Southeast Asia and to work with the US and other international actors to support, to the greatest extent possible, regional governments and institutions that are seen as barriers to the spread of Islamic extremism.

Chapter 4

Muslim separatism in the Philippines and Thailand

The expression of political Islam in the Philippines and Thailand is significantly different from its manifestation in Muslim-majority countries. It reflects the disaffection of the Muslim populations in areas that were once independent political entities, but are now part of non-Muslim majority states. This discontent, which broke out in armed separatist rebellions in the 1970s, is fed by the socio-economic and political grievances of marginalised populations with a strong sense of group identity, defined in Islamic terms. A similar pattern applies in the Indonesian province of Aceh, except that the Acehnese insurgency has taken place within a Muslim-majority country. In both the Philippines and Thailand, although the conflict derives essentially from indigenous causes, it has acquired an international dimension as the separatists established links with Islamic radicals in other parts of the Muslim world.

Mindanao: land of unfulfilled promises

During a visit on the eve of elections in 1986, future President Corazon Aquino described Mindanao as a 'land of unfulfilled promises, a war zone, a land forced into fratricidal strife, a land where every day Filipino kills brother Filipino, a land of avaricious exploitation'.[1] For the last three decades, successive Philippine governments have attempted to suppress or negotiate with the insurgencies that have flared up in the Muslim areas of the southern Philippines, and to address the underlying causes of the rebellion.

Separatist violence in the Philippines predated the establishment of the present-day republic. It originated in the resistance of the Moros, the Muslims of Mindanao and the Sulu archipelago, to Spanish colonial domination and, subsequently, to the US military administration. The Spanish presence dates back to 1571, when an expedition led by Miguel Lopez de Legaspi arrived in Manila, at the time a Muslim settlement. Over the following decade, the Spaniards took possession of most of Luzon and the Visayas, converting the lowland population to Christianity. Beginning in 1629, Spain established footholds in northern and eastern Mindanao and the Zamboanga peninsula, but failed to win control of the rest of Mindanao. Until the end of the nineteenth century, the sultanates in Sulu (Jolo) and Maguindanao fought intermittent wars against the Spanish and conducted independent foreign relations with the British and the Dutch. The Sulu sultanate declined after the mid-nineteenth century, when the Spanish began to use steam-powered warships against the Moros, but Sulu was not made a Spanish protectorate until 1876.

In the course of their struggle against the Spanish colonial authorities, the Moros developed their own unique concept of *jihad*, called *parang sabil* in the Tausug dialect. This involved suicide missions by individuals whom the Spaniards called *juramentados* (literally 'those who had taken an oath'). The suicide-attack ritual involved elaborate preparation of the body in order that the individual might appear before God in the most favourable light. Custom required a solemn conference with the candidate's parents. After a family council, candidates were granted the sultan's permission to engage in holy war. They were then turned over to the imam for organisation and instruction. Prayers were offered, and each candidate swore an oath on the Koran. The candidate was then clothed in a white robe called the *jubba*, and crowned with a white turban. To the waist was attached a charm (an *anting-anting*), to ward off the blows of the enemy. Following his death, the *juramentado*'s body was washed again and wrapped in a white cloth for burial. If the enemy was vanquished in the attack and the *juramentado* escaped with his life, it was believed that he would enter Paradise 40 years after the battle. Attacks by *juramentados* proved a terrifying weapon against the Spanish, and later the Americans.[2]

After the Spanish–American war of April–August 1898, Mindanao was transferred to the US together with the rest of the Philippines, and the American authorities established direct rule over the south. Moro resistance was suppressed and a policy of assimilating the south into the larger Christian-dominated Philippines was attempted.[3] Slavery and polygamy were abolished (at least in law), and reforms such as government schools and a US-style judicial system were introduced. Christians from other parts of the Philippines were encouraged to settle. The ethnic and religious balance was altered – from an overall Muslim majority in Mindanao and the Sulu archipelago at the end of the nineteenth century to less than 17% of the population today – and bitter conflicts emerged over land.

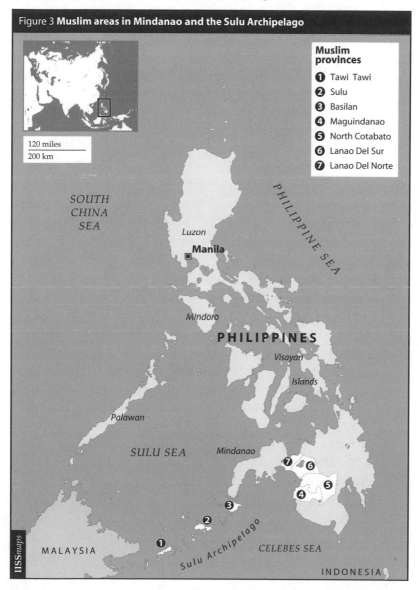

Figure 3 **Muslim areas in Mindanao and the Sulu Archipelago**

Muslim provinces
1. Tawi Tawi
2. Sulu
3. Basilan
4. Maguindanao
5. North Cotabato
6. Lanao Del Sur
7. Lanao Del Norte

120 miles
200 km

SOUTH CHINA SEA

PHILIPPINE SEA

Luzon

Manila

Mindoro

PHILIPPINES

Visayan Islands

Palawan

SULU SEA

Mindanao

MALAYSIA

Sulu Archipelago

CELEBES SEA

INDONESIA

IISSmaps

Since independence in 1946, these resentments have been compounded by government policies that have largely ignored local cultural, religious and political traditions. Inequitable economic policies and uneven investment flows, which mainly benefited the north, exacerbated disparities between Catholics and Muslims, fuelling local alienation and feelings of deprivation. According to a source critical of the Philippine government, major industrial projects in northern Mindanao, such as the National Steel Company mill west of Iligan City, mostly employ Christian migrants from the Visayas, despite official rules about hiring locally.[4]

The main Moro separatist organisations: the MNLF and the MILF

The Moro insurgency began after President Ferdinand Marcos declared martial law in September 1972. Attempts to disarm civilians were viewed by the Moros as an attack on their traditional rights, and the Moro National Liberation Front (MNLF), chaired by Nur Misuari, an ethnic Tausug and a professor at the University of the Philippines, began asserting leadership of the Moro cause. The MNLF's objective was an independent Bangsamoro Republic on Mindanao, Basilan, Sulu and Palawan. Non-Muslims who supported the Moro cause would be entitled to be part of the future republic. The MNLF did not find international support, except from Libya and the government of the Malaysian state of Sabah. In 1975, it abandoned its secessionist goal and entered into protracted negotiations with the Philippine government over an autonomous area for the Moros within the framework of the republic.[5]

In the late 1970s and early 1980s, the MNLF leadership was challenged by two splinter movements: the Banga Moro Liberation Organisation (BMLO), organised by two traditional leaders living as expatriates in Saudi Arabia; and the Maguindanao-led MNLF-Salamat faction, later renamed the Moro Islamic Liberation Front (MILF). The BMLO failed to secure broad support among the Moros and eventually collapsed, but the MILF has gone on to become a significance force in Mindanao. The MILF was founded by Salamat Hashim, the former vice-chairman of the MNLF Central Committee. Salamat had received extensive religious training at Cairo's al-Azhar University, and later lived in Libya, Saudi Arabia and Pakistan.[6] There, he came under the influence of the Islamist ideologues Sayyid

Qutb and Abu A'la Mawdudi.[7] The MILF presented itself as the vanguard of the Islamic revolution in Mindanao. It advocated a return to 'the fold of Islam' and the Islamisation of 'all aspects of life' of the Moro people.[8]

The MILF is currently the largest of the Moro separatist movements, with an armed strength estimated at between 8,000 and 15,000. The group claims the ability to mobilise a much larger number. The bulk of its members come from the Maguindanaos in Cotabato, the Maranaos in Lanao del Sur and the Iranos in North Cotabato and Basilan. MILF tactics are classic guerrilla warfare, with hit-and-run attacks and ambushes. Generally, the group has not mounted indiscriminate attacks against civilians and non-combatants, though when faced with financial difficulties it has allegedly engaged in kidnapping, drug-trafficking and extortion. (The group denies this, and charges that those responsible are common criminals whom the government tries to label as MILF for propaganda purposes.) The MILF also runs legitimate businesses, and receives some of the funds disbursed by Muslim charities.[9]

During the 1970s and 1980s, Libya was the key sponsor and primary source of funds and weapons for both the MNLF and MILF. After the Iranian revolution, Misuari visited Tehran, and the Ayatollah Khomeini prayed openly for the success of the Muslim revolutionary struggle in the Philippines. Iran imposed an oil embargo against the Philippines in November 1979 to protest against the Marcos government's treatment of Philippine Muslims, an important political victory for the MNLF. The Iranians also tried to broker a reconciliation between Misuari and Salamat, but failed to interest the latter, who was at the time under Egyptian influence.[10]

After Libyan funding declined in the mid-1990s, the MILF turned to other sources of external financing, including al-Qaeda. This linkage was facilitated by the participation of MILF volunteers in the Afghan war. During the Soviet occupation of Afghanistan, the MILF sent between 500 and 700 fighters to Pakistan to receive military training and to fight. Mohammed Jamal Khalifa, bin Laden's brother-in-law and agent in the Philippines, apparently began to channel money covertly to the MILF in the early 1990s. At the time, Khalifa was the regional director of the Saudi-based International Islamic Relief Organisation (IIRO), which operated extensively throughout the Muslim world. Al-Qaeda also placed a large number of instructors in MILF military camps to train not only MILF fighters, but also members of Indonesian and Malaysian jihadist groups.[11] According to the authorities in Singapore, in 1997 the MILF allowed the Jemaah Islamiyah to set up its own training camp ('Camp Hudaybiyya'), run by Indonesians and closed to other trainees.[12]

The search for peace in Mindanao

In December 1976, the Marcos government and the MNLF negotiated the 'Tripoli Agreement' under the auspices of the Organisation of the Islamic Conference (OIC). The agreement called for the establishment of a Muslim autonomous region comprising 13 provinces in Mindanao and Sulu. Although the agreement was not implemented, it became the benchmark for future negotiations between Manila and the Moros.[13] The Marcos government also enacted the Code of Muslim Personal Laws, which recognised Islamic civil law as part of Philippine national law and made it applicable to Muslims regardless of their place of residence.

After Marcos was deposed in 1986, Corazon Aquino's administration began negotiations on Moro autonomy with the MNLF, but these failed because of opposition by factions within the Manila government and differences among the Moros.[14] In 1996, the government of Fidel Ramos signed a peace agreement with the MNLF, known as the Davao Consensus. As a result, Misuari was appointed chairman of the Southern Philippines Council for Peace and Development (SPCPD), an executive body representing the three major ethno-religious communities in Mindanao: Christians, Muslims and indigenous Lumads. Misuari was later elected governor of the Autonomous Region of Muslim Mindanao (ARMM), comprising four non-contiguous Muslim-majority provinces: Sulu, Tawi Tawi, Maguindanao and Lanao del Sur. These four provinces opted to be included in the ARMM in a plebiscite in 1989 covering 17 provinces considered the traditional homeland of the Moros. A Special Zone of Peace and Development (SZOPAD) was also established, covering 14 provinces and nine cities in the south. However, The MILF rejected the agreement because it failed to establish an independent state in those areas where the Moros were still a majority.

Despite these moves, the underlying conditions that led to the outbreak of the insurgency remained.[15] The ARMM has done little to improve the lives of ordinary people; its government is inefficient, wasteful and corrupt.[16] In April 2001, the MNLF Central Committee ousted Misuari as chairman, and the central government subsequently replaced him as chairman of the SPCPD with an MNLF rival. Misuari launched a rebellion to forestall the election of a Manila-backed rival as ARMM govenor, then fled to the Malaysian state of Sabah where he was arrested and handed over to the Philippine authorities.[17]

The rise and decline of Abu Sayyaf

The emergence of Abu Sayyaf ('Father of the Sword') in the early 1990s represented a further radicalisation of the fringes of the Moro separatist movement. The group was headed by Abdurajak Janjalani until his death in a clash with police on Basilan island in December 1998. Abdurajak was a veteran of the Afghan war, where he fought with a *mujahideen* group under Abdul Rasul Abu Sayyaf. When the Soviets withdrew from Afghanistan in 1989, Abdurajak returned to Basilan island. There, together with some younger MNLF cadres who were opposed to the MNLF's policy of negotiation, he established the Al Harakatul al-Islamiya or Islamic Movement, commonly known as Abu Sayyaf. By all accounts a charismatic personality, Abdurajak attracted to his movement young Muslims returning from Islamic studies in Saudi Arabia, Libya, Pakistan and Egypt, as well as local militants.[18]

The original goal of Abu Sayyaf was an independent theocratic state in the southern Philippines, but unlike the MNLF and the MILF the group saw its national objective as tied to a global effort to assert the dominance of Islam through armed struggle.[19] Abdurajak had developed strong links to radicals in Afghanistan, including bin Laden. Bin Laden's brother-in-law Khalifa helped to establish Abu Sayyaf, but there is little evidence of a continued relationship with al-Qaeda.

The group's first recorded operation was in 1991, when it attacked a military checkpoint on the outskirts of the town of Isabela on Basilan island. The group was responsible for a series of kidnappings and attacks from 1993 to 1995, when a ceasefire between the government and the MNLF was holding throughout much of Mindanao. In 1996, bolstered by renegade MNLF guerrillas, Abu Sayyaf attacked the town of Ipil, robbing banks and setting the town ablaze before fleeing with several hostages. The raid left 54 people dead and hundreds wounded.[20]

With Abdurajak's death in 1998, the group lost much of its ideological impetus and became little more than a criminal enterprise. In March 2000, it kidnapped 58 students and teachers from a school on Basilan; in April 2000 it took 21 hostages, including ten foreign tourists, from a diving resort in the Malaysian state of Sabah. The kidnap netted Abu Sayyaf $20 million in ransom money reportedly paid by Libya. In May 2001, another group of hostages, including three Americans, was seized and taken to the group's Basilan stronghold. The kidnap provoked a large-scale military operation that resulted in the death of a number of terrorists and hostages, as well as additional kidnaps. Subsequently, Khaddafy Janjalani, who had succeeded his brother Abdurajak as leader of the group, unsuccessfully attempted to engage the Manila government in negotiations.[21]

The Philippines in the war on terrorism

President Gloria Macapagal Arroyo, who took office in January 2001, saw the war on terrorism as an opportunity to engage the US in the government's military campaign against Abu Sayyaf. Arroyo had criticised her predecessor, Joseph Estrada, for succumbing to 'Malaysian and European pleas to hold the troops back', and for allowing Libya to arrange a ransom deal with Abu Sayyaf.[22] Abu Sayyaf's kidnapping of two Americans (and its murder of a third) and its links to bin Laden provided a common target for the Philippine and US governments. In late 2001, Manila allowed US forces to overfly Philippine airspace and use airfields as transit points in support of *Operation Enduring Freedom* in Afghanistan. The US in turn provided anti-terrorism training and advice, and deployed military personnel, including 160 US Army Special Forces troops, to Zamboanga in Mindanao and on Basilan.[23] Given the Philippines' predominantly Catholic population, Arroyo's position did not expose the government to the same pressures as its counterparts in Indonesia and Malaysia. Nevertheless, the presence of US forces is a sensitive issue, and the decision to accept American trainers was a major political gamble.

The campaign against Abu Sayyaf has seriously degraded the group's capabilities. From a peak of 1,000 fighters in the mid-1990s, it has dwindled to a few hundred. They are now scattered and on the run, and unable to launch the kind of large-scale kidnaps of the past. According to the government, Abu Sayyaf is also losing its hold over the people of Basilan island. Whereas in the past the group was able to obtain or compel support, there is now greater confidence in the government's ability to protect the population. Along with military operations, the government is improving conditions on Basilan, providing medical services, upgrading roads and rehabilitating an airfield and a wharf.[24] At the beginning of 2003, Abu Sayyaf appeared to have regrouped on the mountainous island of Jolo (Sulu), where some of the leaders had fled.[25]

The focus on Abu Sayyaf has been controversial since the MILF has the strongest links to the Jemaah Islamiyah network, and through Jemaah Islamiyah to al-Qaeda. It is also the strongest of the Moro separatist groups. In 2000, Estrada declared all-out war against the MILF, and scored a significant success with the capture of its headquarters, Camp Abubakar, in July 2000. However, the MILF's military strength was not destroyed. On assuming office, Arroyo reversed Estrada's approach and declared herself ready to resume talks. A ceasefire, brokered by Malaysia, was signed in August 2001. In a related development, also brokered by Malaysia, the MNLF and the MILF signed a reunification agreement meant to strengthen the Moros' negotiating position.[26]

In early 2003, negotiations took place in Kuala Lumpur between the Philippine government and the MILF; meanwhile, there was intense fighting between government and MILF forces in the province of North Cotabato. In mid-February, Philippine army troops overran an important MILF stronghold near the town of Pikit.[27] On 4 March, a terrorist attack on the airport in Davao, the largest city in Mindanao, left 17 people dead and over a hundred injured. The MILF denied involvement in the bombing, but Davao's mayor stated that the police had evidence connecting the bombing to the MILF.[28]

Thailand: the waning of Muslim separatism

Two separatist organisations, the Patani United Liberation Organisation (PULO) and the smaller New PULO, were active in southern Thailand during the 1990s, but have since declined as the result of effective government action and the end of support from associates in Malaysia. PULO's secessionist struggle began in 1968. The group had an armed wing, the Patani United Liberation Army (PULA), which claimed responsibility for bomb and arson attacks against government establishments and perceived symbols of Thai cultural domination in the south, such as schools and Buddhist temples.[29] The

New PULO emerged as a dissident faction in 1995, but two years later the two organisations formed a tactical alliance in an attempt to refocus attention on the 'southern question'. Operating under the name of Bersatu (Solidarity), they carried out a series of coordinated attacks against state workers, law-enforcement personnel, local-government officials and schoolteachers.[30]

The Thai government complained that the separatists were taking advantage of safe havens in the Malaysian state of Kelantan, and that this support could not have been extended without the sanction of the state's PAS government. Bangkok warned that closer cross-border economic ties would be curtailed if cooperation against the separatists was not stepped up.[31] Mahathir acceded to Thai demands and personally sanctioned joint police raids against secessionists thought to be hiding in northern Malaysia. The resulting collaboration led to the arrest of several PULO and New PULO leaders in early 1998. This was a major blow to both groups, and encouraged many cadres to lay down their arms; in the months that followed, more than 900 militants from PULO, New PULO and smaller groups voluntarily joined a government-sponsored 'rehabilitation' programme.[32] Several key separatist leaders fled abroad.[33]

Over the past decade, the Thai government has taken significant steps to address the underlying causes of Muslim discontent by improving social and economic conditions in the south.[34] The city of Pattani has become a major economic and educational centre, and opportunities have opened up for Muslims at all levels of the public administration. Muslims have risen to cabinet level in recent Thai governments; one, Surin Pitsuwan, served as foreign minister and is one of Southeast Asia's most prominent political figures.[35]

Notwithstanding these improvements, it is still too early to conclude that armed separatism is at an end in southern Thailand. Malaysia might in future exert pressure on Thailand by taking a less active role in blunting Malay sympathies for southern Thai Muslims. Southern Thailand also remains underdeveloped relative to other parts of the country, and perceptions of linguistic and religious discrimination persist.[36]

Conclusion

Among the Moros in the southern Philippines and the Malay Muslims of southern Thailand, the Islamic resurgence took the form of resistance to the domination of non-Muslim national majorities and the central governments that represented them. This resistance was manifested in the defence of the cultural and political identity of the Muslim communities, in its extreme form through armed separatist movements. Although this resistance was expressed in an Islamic idiom, it had deeper roots in the history of relations between these minorities and the national power centre. The Islamic component of Moro and Pattani separatism nonetheless has important implications in that Islam was the nexus that tied indigenous movements to wider international networks of support. These networks are examined in the following chapter.

Chapter 5

Terrorist networks in Southeast Asia[1]

The Jemaah Islamiyah network

The presence of terrorist networks linked to al-Qaeda in Southeast Asia surfaced with the arrests in Malaysia and Singapore of militants associated with Jemaah Islamiyah. The key figures in this regional network were Indonesian clerics who had settled in Malaysia in the 1990s: Mohamad Iqbal Abdur Rahman alias Abu Jibril; the aforementioned Abu Bakar Bashir alias Abdus Samad; and Riduan Isamuddin alias Hambali. Part of the network was uncovered in May and June 2001, with the arrests of 25 suspected KMM members. Among the detainees were Nik Adli Nik Aziz and Indonesian cleric Abu Jibril. Abu Jibril is believed to have played a key role in the KMM, and in arranging meetings between al-Qaeda representatives and Indonesian militant groups.

In December 2001, the Malaysian authorities arrested 13 members of a new wing of the KMM. One, a US-educated former Malaysian Army captain, Yazid Sufaat, was arrested while returning from Afghanistan by way of Thailand. At Hambali's direction, Sufaat had hosted two of the 11 September hijackers, Khalid Al Mihdhar and Nawaf Al Hazmi, at his home in Kuala Lumpur during their visit to Malaysia in January 2000. Sufaat established al-Qaeda front companies in Malaysia, one of which, Infocus Technology, hired Zacharias Moussaoui as a 'marketing consultant' and helped him to obtain a US visa.[2] In early 2003 Moussaoui, the only suspect indicted for the 11 September attacks, was on trial in the US. According to the Malaysian authorities, Sufaat also arranged for the purchase of four tons of ammonium nitrate (four times the amount used in the Oklahoma City bombing).

Thirteen alleged members of a Jemaah Islamiyah cell in Singapore were arrested in December 2001. According to the authorities, the group had relatively well-developed plans to use truck bombs to attack the American and Israeli embassies, the Australian and British high commissions and commercial buildings housing US firms. There were also plans to attack a shuttle bus carrying US military personnel, and US naval vessels in Singapore. Jemaah Islamiyah also considered attacks against Singaporean targets, including water pipelines, Changi airport and radar station, and the Ministry of Defence.

Interrogation of the suspects arrested in Malaysia and Singapore revealed that al-Qaeda had worked actively in Southeast Asia to cultivate radical Muslims, that it had succeeded in establishing an extensive regional network and that it had provided its members with training and funds.[3] The members of the Singapore cell had been recruited in religious classes run by the cell's leader, Ibrahim Maidin, a religious teacher recruited by Abu Jibril. Of the 13, at least eight had gone to Afghanistan for training in al-Qaeda camps. The network's Malaysia-based leadership had made covert arrangements for their travel to Afghanistan, including false documentation showing that they had been accepted by a religious school in Pakistan. The men travelled by road to Kuala Lumpur and then flew to Karachi in Pakistan. On arrival in Pakistan, they were moved to a safe house, from where they and other trainees were transported in batches to al-Qaeda camps in Afghanistan. The training included the use of AK-47 assault rifles and mortars, and military tactics. A letter in an encrypted computer disk, found in the possession of Mohamed Khalim bin Jaffar, one of the Jemaah Islamiyah cell members arrested by the authorities, nominated two militants for specialised training in ambush/assassination, sniper skills or bomb-making.[4] After the fall of the Taliban regime in Afghanistan, a videotape of the reconnaissance conducted by members of the terrorist network in Singapore was found in the home of Osama bin Laden's military adviser, Mohammed Atef, in Kabul (Atef was killed in the US bombing).

The investigation showed a sophisticated regional network linking groups in Singapore, Malaysia, Indonesia and the Philippines (see Figure 4). The organisation consists of three or four districts or territories called *mantiqi*. The first covers peninsular Malaysia and

Singapore; the second Java; and the third the southern Philippines, the Malaysian state of Sabah on Borneo and the Indonesian island of Sulawesi.[5] A fourth *mantiqi* is reportedly being organised in Australia and the Indonesian province of Papua.[6]

Each *mantiqi* is made up of several branches, or *wakalah*. The Singapore network was headed by a leader (*qoaid wakalah*), and organised into several functional cells or *fiah* responsible for fund-raising, religious work, security and operations. The network reported to a regional leadership council (*syura*) in Malaysia, headed by Hambali after the arrest of Jibril and other militants in 2001. The group avoided mainstream Muslim organisations and kept tight operational security, using code words and code names for communication. Members of one of the operational cells started exploring terrorist targets in Singapore as early as 1997; two well-developed plans were reported by one of the cell's members to the al-Qaeda leadership in Afghanistan between August 1999 and April 2000. The al-Qaeda leaders showed interest, but did not pursue the plans.[7]

In September 2002, the Singaporean authorities announced the arrest the previous month of another 21 suspects; 19 were alleged members of Jemaah Islamiyah, and two had links to the MILF. At least 14 had undergone military training in Malaysia, the Philippines and Afghanistan. The Singaporean authorities identified Hambali as the mastermind. A small group of Malaysians based in Johor state provided the leadership and worked directly with Hambali. The militants hoped to stir up ethnic strife and make Muslims respond to calls for a *jihad*, which would in turn create the conditions to overthrow the Malaysian government and establish an Islamic state. According to the Singaporean authorities, Jemaah Islamiyah had formed an alliance with the MILF and a militant group based in southern Thailand's Narithiwat province, providing for cooperation in training, arms procurement, funding and the coordination of operations.[8]

Further evidence of al-Qaeda's connections in Southeast Asia emerged from the trial in Madrid of eight alleged members of an al-Qaeda cell in Spain. One of the eight, Luis Jose Gallant Gonzalez alias Yusuf Gallant, received military training at an Indonesian camp. Parlindungan Siregar alias Parlin, who reportedly worked in the Laskar Jihad organisation, was named as his contact. (As of early 2003, Siregar had not been found.) When Gallant Gonzalez was arrested at his Madrid home, the police found guns, ammunition, knives, a bulletproof vest, forged identification documents, travel documents to Indonesia and photographs apparently taken at the Indonesian training camp. The camp in question was near Poso in Central Sulawesi, an area that saw communal conflict from 2000 to 2002. According to the *Jakarta Post*, the camp received about 50 new recruits every two or three months. Automatic weapons were available, their storage and distribution supervised by 'men who spoke Arabic'. The Poso camp was abandoned around July 2001.[9]

Laskar Jihad was believed to have links to al-Qaeda. After 11 September 2001, however, the group's leader Jaafar tried hard to distance his organisation from bin Laden and his network. Jaafar criticised bin Laden's understanding of Islam and told the press that he had turned down an offer of money and training from bin Laden's representatives. Nevertheless, there are reports of al-Qaeda trainers with Laskar Jihad and of arms shipments to the group from the Filipino group Abu Sayyaf.[10]

Bashir and Hambali

The backgrounds of the two leading personalities in Jemaah Islamiyah, Abu Bakar Bashir and Hambali, cast light on the evolution of Islamic

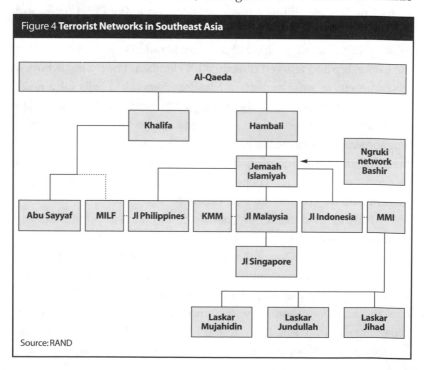

Figure 4 **Terrorist Networks in Southeast Asia**

Source: RAND

extremism and terrorism in Southeast Asia. In the late 1970s, Bashir and Abdullah Sungkar, an Islamic figure associated with the DDII, established an Islamic boarding school, the Pesantren Al-Mukmin, in the village of Ngruki in Central Java. This formed the basis of what has been called the Ngruki network. The group's commitment to the establishment of an Islamic state apparently drew heavily on the experience of the Darul Islam rebellion in West Java in the late 1940s and 1950s.[11]

In 1978, Bashir and Sungkar were arrested for belonging to a clandestine organisation, promoting *jihad* and refusing to acknowledge the primacy of the Indonesian constitution and the state philosophy of Pancasila. They were convicted and sentenced to nine years in prison. After their release on appeal in 1982, Bashir established a network of cells in Central Java, whose members were required to swear an oath of allegiance (*bayat*) to him. In 1985, the Indonesian Supreme Court reimposed the original nine-year sentence. When their rearrest appeared imminent, Bashir, Sungkar and other members of the Ngruki network fled to Malaysia.[12] There, Sungkar established an Islamic school near the city of Johor, the al-Tarbiyah Luqmanul Hakiem, which became the recruitment centre for their network. Bashir and Sungkar's operation apparently served as a way-station for Indonesians and Malaysians en route to Pakistan and Afghanistan. Sungkar travelled to the Afghan border region in the early 1990s, where he met bin Laden and pledged *bayat* to him, effectively submerging his organisation into the al-Qaeda network.[13]

The key link between Sungkar and Bashir and al-Qaeda was Hambali, an experienced al-Qaeda operative who had fought against the Soviets in Afghanistan, and one of the few non-Arabs to have become a member of al-Qaeda's *shura* (supreme council). In the early 1990s, the three began to establish the transnational network that became Jemaah Islamiyah. The network sent members to Pakistan and Afghanistan, developed contacts in the Middle East and Europe and established close links to al-Gama'a al-Islamiya, an Egyptian group which later merged with al-Qaeda.[14]

After the fall of Suharto in May 1998, Bashir, Sungkar and other exiles returned to Indonesia (Sungkar died soon thereafter of natural causes). After the June 2001 arrest of KMM militants, the Malaysian authorities cited Bashir as a key member of the KMM and requested his extradition; the Indonesian authorities declined to comply, citing insufficient evidence. In August 2000, Bashir was appointed head of the advisory council of the Majelis Mujahidin Indonesia (MMI), a coalition of militant Islamic groups based in Yogyakarta. According to Indonesian intelligence agencies, the MMI gives political direction to an armed group, Laskar Jundullah, in Maluku and Sulawesi. Laskar Jundullah's leader is Agus Dwikarna, who is also secretary of the MMI's Executive Board and an official in the Crisis Centre Committee (Kompak), an organisation established by the DDII to distribute funds from the Middle East in areas of conflict in eastern Indonesia.[15] One Southeast Asian intelligence service believes that Kompak is a conduit for al-Qaeda funds. Dwikarna is also the regional head of a Saudi charity, the al-Haramain Foundation, which US investigators believe is a significant source of funding for terrorist groups in Southeast Asia.[16]

Dwikarna and two other Indonesians, Tamsil Linrung and Abdul Jamal Balfas, were arrested at Manila's Ninoy Aquino International Airport in March 2002 after security personnel discovered plastic explosives and detonators in their luggage. According to the Philippine authorities, the three were connected to Jemaah Islamiyah; together with a Thai accomplice who remained at large, they apparently met MILF contacts in the southern port city of General Santos. Linrung, a former treasurer of the mainstream Indonesian political party PAN, was released after heavy lobbying by the Indonesian government and political leaders. Dwikarna denied wrongdoing and asserted that he and his companions had been set up by Indonesian intelligence. Nevertheless, he was tried in the Philippines and sentenced to 17 years in prison.[17]

Less is known about Hambali, who is probably the most wanted man in Southeast Asia. Like Bashir, he was part of the group of religious activists who went to Malaysia in the 1980s during Suharto's crackdown on Islamic militants. After taking part in the war against Soviet forces in Afghanistan, Hambali returned to Malaysia in the early 1990s, where he was part of the leadership of Jemaah Islamiyah and the KMM. After 1993, he reportedly lived in Sunggai Manggis, a town about 50 kilometres south of Kuala Lumpur, and home to a large Indonesian immigrant community.[18] He travelled to Afghanistan in October 2001, but is believed to have since returned to Southeast Asia.

In the early 1990s, Hambali and Khalid Sheikh Mohammed, a senior al-Qaeda operative arrested in Pakistan in March 2003, established a network in the Philippines. The US Federal Bureau of

Investigation (FBI) named Mohammed, also known as Salim Ali, as a planner of the 11 September attacks. He is believed to be the uncle of another key member of the Philippine cell, Ramzi Yousef, who was convicted of plotting the 1993 bombing of the World Trade Center. Yousef and another member of the cell, Wali Khan Amin Shah, established a shell company, the Bermuda Trading Company, to purchase chemicals for planned bomb attacks on US airliners and the planned assassination of Pope John Paul II during his visit to the Philippines in 1995. Another conspirator, Abdul Hakim Murad, a Pakistani trained as a pilot, reportedly intended to hijack a commercial airliner in the US and crash it into the Central Intelligence Agency (CIA) headquarters near Washington.[19]

The Ramzi Yousef cell was broken up when Yousef and another conspirator accidentally set fire to Yousef's apartment in Manila when they were mixing chemicals to make bombs. Yousef fled the Philippines, but was arrested in Pakistan in 1995 and extradited to the US, where he was convicted of terrorism in two separate trials. He is serving a life sentence. Wali Khan Amin Shah was arrested in Malaysia in 1995 and turned over to the US, where he has cooperated with the authorities.[20] Khalil Sheikh Mohammed remained at large until his arrest in March 2003.

These arrests did not end the international terrorist presence in the Philippines. An Indonesian Jemaah Islamiyah operative and former Ngruki student, Fathur Rohman al-Ghozi, who was arrested in the Philippines in January 2001, travelled between Malaysia, Singapore, Indonesia and the Philippines, and made contact with the MILF. Rohman al-Ghozi is believed to be responsible for the bomb attacks in Manila in December 2000.[21] Information provided by Rohman al-Ghozi led the Philippine authorities to arrest Hussain Ramos, who also went by the aliases Ali Ramos and Abu Ali, in July 2002. Ramos admitted helping to procure the explosives earmarked for the attacks on the US Embassy and other targets in Singapore.[22]

International terrorist links to the MILF

There is considerable evidence of links between the MILF, Jemaah Islamiyah and Indonesian terrorists. Two of the individuals detained in the first wave of arrests in Singapore in December 2001 and another two in the group arrested in August 2002 had been involved in training at MILF camps, and in fund-raising activities for the MILF.[23]

Omar al-Faruq, the senior al-Qaeda operative captured in Indonesia in 2001, spent time in Camp Abubakar, the main MILF base in Mindanao.[24] After the Philippine Army captured the camp in July 2000, the MILF sent militants for training at the camp at Poso that was also used by al-Qaeda. A bomb attack in August 2000 outside the home of the Philippine ambassador to Indonesia, which killed two people and severely injured the diplomat, is believed to have been carried out by the Indonesian branch of Jemaah Islamiyah at the behest of the MILF.[25]

The ASEAN response

The links among extremist and terrorist groups in Southeast Asia and beyond are dense and widespread. With the increased understanding of the regional nature of the threat has come increased cooperation and information exchanges among the intelligence services of Singapore, Malaysia, the Philippines and Indonesia. Association of South-East Asian Nations (ASEAN) home affairs ministers met in Kuala Lumpur at the end of May 2002, and agreed to take concrete steps to strengthen counter-terrorist cooperation. In August 2002, ASEAN foreign ministers met US Secretary of State Colin Powell in Brunei, where they agreed to establish a region-wide intelligence network, take steps to block the flow of terrorist funds and tighten border controls.[26] While collective action against terrorism faces formidable obstacles, including porous and poorly-controlled borders, weaknesses in intelligence and law-enforcement institutions and, in some countries, a political reluctance to admit the gravity of the threat, enhanced intelligence-sharing has produced notable successes.

Conclusion

The 11 September attacks and the onset of the global war on terrorism changed the political landscape in Southeast Asia in fundamental ways. First, threat perceptions changed. Armed extremists and terrorist groups were operating in Southeast Asia before 11 September, but their activities were considered limited in scope. Now these groups are seen as more extensive and linked in varying ways to widespread regional and international networks. There is now a greater understanding in the West and among Southeast Asian governments of the challenges that terrorism and radical Islam pose to regional security, as well as greater political will to confront them.

Second, policy priorities changed, both in the West and among regional governments and political actors. There have been significant changes in US policy towards the region, with issues that loomed large in the US bilateral relationship with Malaysia and Indonesia before 11 September receding. Thus, the US resumed some cooperation with the Indonesian military, a decision announced barely a week after the attacks, and lifted the embargo on the sale of non-lethal military items. In July 2002, the Senate Appropriations Committee removed restrictions on funding military training for Indonesia that had been in effect, in one way or another, since 1993. The following month, Powell visited Jakarta, where he stated that the US expected to give Indonesia a $50m multi-year assistance package for counter-terrorism and law enforcement.[1] In February 2003, the US Congress passed the appropriations law, without restrictions on the funding of military education and training for Indonesia. An amendment to remove the funding for Indonesia proposed by Senator Russ Feingold, Democrat from Wisconsin, failed in the Senate, 36-61. The availability of US Foreign Military Financing

(FMF) for Indonesia remained conditional on accountability for human rights violations in East Timor, and on transparency in Indonesian military receipts and expenditures. Similarly, the high level of US assistance to the Philippines is in marked contrast to Washington's relative disinterest in Manila's military requirements before 11 September. US Foreign Military Financing (FMF) for the Philippines increased from $2m in fiscal year 2001 to $19m in fiscal year 2002. In addition, the US allocated $10m for the transfer of defence equipment and services to re-equip, transport and train the Philippine military, and transferred significant amounts of excess military equipment, including transport aircraft, naval patrol craft, trucks and rifles. The Philippines has become the world's third-largest recipient of US International Military Education and Training (IMET) funding, with $1.3m in fiscal year 2002.

The future of Southeast Asian Islam

The challenges that religious extremism and terrorism pose in Southeast Asia are too complex to be amenable to simple solutions. The most practical approach to the formulation of an effective policy response is to disaggregate the problem into its components. Two broad classes of related but distinct threats can be identified: international terrorism; and the destabilisation of moderate regional governments by Islamic extremists.

International terrorists and domestic extremists operating in Southeast Asia have different agendas and strategies. The international terrorist networks focus on US and international targets, while domestic extremists are driven largely by internal factors and pursue domestic goals. The separatists are in a different category, although their methods and ideologies may be similar. There are, of course, extensive links among these groups. Since many share the same ideological orientation and biases, international terrorists have found it relatively easy to infiltrate and influence domestic radical groups and, through them, mainstream Muslim organisations.

The critical long-term issue in Muslim-majority countries such as Indonesia and Malaysia is whether a moderate or a militant version of political Islam will prevail. While this is a 'domestic' issue, it has implications for counter-terrorism, since a government dominated or influenced by radical Islamists is more likely to be sympathetic with the goals of terrorist groups and more tolerant of their activities. Radical Islamists are a minority in Southeast Asian countries, as elsewhere in the

Muslim world. Accordingly, the main obstacle to the inroads of radical political Islam comes from the mainstream Muslim groups themselves. However, there are political and psychological obstacles to effective action by moderates against radicals. In Indonesia in particular, the secular government and moderate Muslim leaders have not fully mobilised this latent source of support to regain control of the political and ideological agenda. The danger is that, without an effective political-education campaign by moderate Muslims, the radicals, albeit in a minority, might be able to set the parameters of political debate.

There are indications that Indonesian moderates are beginning such a mobilisation. Nahdlatul Ulama and Muhammadiyah leaders have appeared together in public to emphasise that Islam does not advocate violence and to warn against the misuse of religion. An increasing number of Muslim scholars are seeking ways to separate Islam from politics, following the 'New Islamic Theology of Politics' introduced in the 1980s by Nurcholish Madjid. This school of thought contends that Muslims are not obliged to support Islamic parties; its watchword is 'Islam yes, Islamic party no'. It also seeks to improve educational opportunities for Muslims so that they can become part of the globalised economy. Some Indonesian Muslim leaders, such as former President Wahid, Muhammadiyah chairman Ahmad Syafii Maarif and a younger generation of leaders, are among the spokesmen for this school of 'New Muslim Thinking'.

One of the conditions generating Islamic extremism in countries otherwise as different as Indonesia and Cambodia is the breakdown of state authority. Therefore, whether the central government succeeds in restoring order and stability, and whether it provides services to the population, will be critical in determining whether Islamic extremism continues to grow. In Indonesia, the upsurge of radical and violent groups to a large extent was the result of the breakdown in state authority after the fall of Suharto, as well as the release of pent-up political tensions built up over three decades. If the government in Jakarta is unable to restore a sense of security, the scope of action for religious and other extremists will continue to expand. Conversely, political and economic stabilisation will reduce opportunities for extremists to dominate political discourse among Muslims, and allow moderate voices to reassert themselves.

As one of the few institutions that cuts across the many divides in Indonesian society, the Indonesian military will play a crucial role.[3]

Despite its shortcomings and the links that some military sectors have with extremist groups, the armed forces as an institution remain committed to Indonesia's secular constitution. However, the military is part of society and is not immune from the forces transforming Indonesia. Over time, continued Islamisation or the coming to power of an Islamic-oriented government could change the religio-political balance within the military institution itself.

In Malaysia, countervailing structural factors can be expected to halt Islamisation before the Islamists reach their goal of a *sharia*-based state. These include:

- the dichotomised character of Malaysian society. Even if all Malays were in agreement on an Islamic state, this would not be acceptable to the non-Muslim half of the population;
- disagreements among Malays themselves as to the type of Islam they would like to see in Malaysia. This disunity is reflected in the divide between UMNO and PAS, and in the differences between modernists and religious traditionalists;
- differences between the eastern and western halves of Malaysia. The two eastern states, Sarawak and Sabah, only joined the Malaysian Federation in 1963 after an acrimonious internal debate. Neither has a Malay majority and neither is hospitable ground for religiously-based politics; and
- the strength of the secular institutions that provide the framework for Malaysian political and economic life.

Over the short to medium term, the balance between fundamentalist political Islam, embodied in PAS, and the modernising version represented by UMNO will be affected by the political transition resulting from Mahathir's retirement in late 2003. If party discipline prevails and UMNO holds together, as seems likely at least in the near term, and particularly if the government is able to reduce the profile of political Islam in education, Malaysia will probably continue on its current trajectory. If UMNO falters, PAS could increase its influence across the 'Malay belt' of northern states, and over the national government, even if it did not dominate the latter. This would exacerbate ethnic and religious divides and increase tensions in Malaysian society, providing more room for extremist movements.

In countries where Muslims are in a minority, such as the Philippines and Thailand, the issue of Islam and politics is framed differently. The question of whether radical or moderate forms of Islam will prevail in Muslim areas remains important, but it is not likely to shape these countries' overall orientation. Instead, the central issue is national reconciliation. The success of such efforts is likely to hinge on the ability of central governments to address discontent by opening up political, social and economic opportunities for minority populations. Doing so does not guarantee an end to terrorism or extremism; the discovery of the network in Singapore is a case in point. However, improving political opportunities and socio-economic conditions in potentially disaffected regions reduces potential popular support for extremist movements.

Thailand appears to be well on the way to ameliorating the problems that generated the insurgency of the 1990s in the southern provinces. The Philippines is another matter. The MILF retains a strong armed presence in the Muslim areas of the south. Since there is little prospect of a military solution, resolving the conflict will require a multi-pronged approach involving good-faith negotiations between the Philippine government and the MILF; a real improvement in economic and social conditions in the Muslim areas; and the restoration of a climate of security for the population, which requires the suppression of politico-criminal groups such as Abu Sayyaf. These are all elements of the government's strategy. Although the MILF is apparently closely linked to the Southeast Asian terrorist network, the government and its international backers have decided not to make these a barrier to negotiation. The question is whether the MILF will be willing to settle for an arrangement short of an independent Moro state, and sever its links with terrorist organisations.

Within the Muslim areas of the Philippines, there has been a remarkable upsurge in civil-society organisations formed specifically to address the problems of poverty and corruption. The first, the Ompia ('Reform') party, was set up in the 1980s by the Maranao *ulama* in Lanao del Sur province in Mindanao. The Ulama League of the Philippines is also active in promoting peace and development. The Magbassa Kita Foundation has developed a literacy programme that is being implemented nationwide. In 1985 its founder, Santanina Rasul, became the first and only Muslim woman to be elected to the Philippine Senate and the first Muslim to be elected in a majority Christian district.[4] There is also a regional dimension to this flourishing of Muslim civil society. In the late 1980s, there was a movement towards regional dialogue on Islam involving Muslim moderates in southern Thailand, Singapore, Malaysia, the Philippines and Indonesia through the Forum of Muslim Social Scientists. This forum may be revived.[5]

The challenge for the West

The challenge for the West is to support the reconsolidation of viable democratic states in Southeast Asia, particularly in Indonesia, and to forge stronger links with what has been called 'civil Islam', the Muslim civil-society groups that advocate moderation and modernity.[6] Indonesia should be the focus of this effort. If Indonesia succeeds in consolidating a pluralistic democracy, it will be the world's third-largest and the largest in the Muslim world. Moderate political Islam as a force in a democratic pluralistic Indonesia could be an antidote to theocratic ideologies and concepts of an intolerant and exclusionist Islamic state.

There is an urgent need for international assistance to 'civil Islam' organisations. Funding for education and cultural programmes run by secular or moderate Muslim organisations should be a priority, to counter the influence of radical Islamic religious schools and institutions. Outside support for such groups, however, is exceedingly sensitive in Islamic countries. Assistance from international sources needs to be channelled in ways appropriate to local circumstances and, to the extent possible, should rely on non-governmental organisations.

A complementary element of this strategy is to deny resources to the extremists. This will be extremely difficult. The poor regulation of banking systems in Southeast Asia and the widespread use of the *hawalah* system hinder the authorities' ability to monitor suspicious financial flows. It is critical that the technical capabilities of Southeast Asian finance ministries and intelligence agencies are strengthened. Members of the international community could bring pressure to bear on governments at the source of these financial flows, such as Saudi Arabia, to ensure that funds go to legitimate organisations in recipient countries.

Assisting economic recovery throughout the region will help to dampen religious extremism. The 1997 economic crisis created widespread hardship and social dislocation, and exacerbated divides among ethnic and religious groups. Improving socio-economic conditions will not necessarily alter the radical minority's determination to strike at the perceived enemies of Islam, but it would reduce support for them among the Muslim community at large. This is particularly true where, as in Mindanao, the Muslim communities' grievances are focused on local issues.

The experience of Maluku, Mindanao and other areas of conflict shows that economic development is unlikely to take place without peace and security. Therefore, an integrated security strategy that strengthens the capabilities of the security forces to enable them to suppress extremist and terrorist groups as well as to engage in civic-action projects is vital. In the Philippines, where their minority status renders relations between Muslim communities and the central government particularly sensitive, it is critically important that the government and its international supporters distinguish between terrorists and extremists, and the Moro people. The negotiation of a fair and durable settlement with the MILF is a requirement for stable peace. With a climate of security as a precondition, the government and its international backers could then address the need for a tangible improvement in economic and social conditions. A programme of technical assistance to improve governance in the ARMM and assistance to civil-society organisations should be priorities for international donors.

The key requirement of an effective long-term strategy for the West is to balance the need to meet the threat of terrorism with the risk that the war on terrorism poses to the stability of moderate Muslim countries. The war on terrorism will continue to have a serious impact on Muslim communities in Southeast Asia, but this need not be destabilising. Much will depend on the efforts of the mainstream Muslim leadership to prevent radicals from hijacking the agenda, and on the success of the US and its allies in making clear to Muslims that the war on terrorism is not a war on Islam. It will be important for the US to demonstrate that its efforts are not directed at strengthening repressive and authoritarian regimes, but at promoting democratic change in the Muslim world. The success of such a project in Southeast Asia could have profound implications for the future of Islam more widely in the Muslim world, and for the shape of the international order in the twenty-first century.

Notes

Introduction

1   For a discussion of Islamisation in Malaysia, see Chandra Muzaffar's important study *Islamic Resurgence in Malaysia* (Kuala Lumpur: Penerbit Fajar Bakti Sdn. Bhd., 1987), pp. 3–6.
2   The most detailed rules of governance from the period of the early caliphs are found in Caliph Ali's instructions to Malik Ashtar, the governor of Egypt, in 795 AD.
3   The caliph (*khalifa*) held the title of commander of the faithful (*amir al-mu'minin*), which has military connotations. For a historical overview of the institution of the caliphate, see H. A. R. Gibb and J. H. Kramers, *Concise Encyclopedia of Islam* (London and Leiden: Brill Academic Publishers, 2001), pp. 236–41.
4   Azyumardi Azra, 'Globalization of Indonesian Muslim Discourse', in Johan Meuleman (ed.), *Islam in the Era of Globalization* (Jakarta: INIS, 2001), p. 45.
5   Mohammad Mohaddessin, *Islamic Fundamentalism* (Washington DC: Seven Locks Press, 2001), pp. 56–57.
6   In the view of some scholars, these movements, with their emphasis on an exclusionist conception of religious identity, were largely responsible for the faltering of a pluralistic worldview in the Islamic world. Muhammad Khalid Masud, 'Religious Identity and Mass Education', in Meuleman (ed.), *Islam in the Era of Globalization*, p. 234.
7   See Robert W. Hefner, 'Muslim Politics in Indonesia After September 11', statement before the US House of Representatives, Foreign Relations Committee, Subcommittee on East Asia and the Pacific, 12 December 2001.

Chapter 1

1   On Nahdlatul Ulama, see Douglas E. Ramage, 'Social Organizations: Nahdlatul Ulama and Pembangunan', in Richard Baker et al. (eds), *Indonesia: The Challenge of Change* (Singapore: Institute of Southeast Asian Studies, 1999).
2   Discussion with Dr Azyumardi Azra, Jakarta, June 2002.
3   Johan Meuleman, 'The Institut Agama Islam Negeri at the Crossroads', in Meuleman (ed.), *Islam in the Era of Globalization*, pp. 283–88. Over 100,000 students are enrolled in the IAIN system.
4   '"Ideology Is Dead" in Politics', *Jakarta Post*, 29 May 2002.

5   Discussion with Dr Nurcholish Madjid, Jakarta, February 2002.

6   The term Salafi derives from *salaf* (ancestors), specifically the first three generations of pious Muslims during and after the revelation of the Koran. Salafis adhere to what they believe was the original practice of Islam in its early years. See Dawat-us-Salafiyyah, http://muttaqun.com/salafiyyah.html.

7   See Hussin Mutalib, *Islam in Malaysia: From Revivalism to Islamic State?* (Singapore: Singapore University Press, 1993), pp. 20–26.

8   Kamarulnizam Abdullah, 'National Security and Malay Unity: The Issue of Radical Religious Elements in Malaysia', *Contemporary Southeast Asia*, vol. 21, no. 2, August 1999, pp. 272–75.

9   Azra, 'Globalization of Indonesian Muslim Discourse', in Meuleman (ed.), *Islam in the Era of Globalization*, pp. 43–44.

10 *The World Factbook*, Malaysia (Washington DC: Central Intelligence Agency, 2002). Malays are defined in the Federal Constitution as those who profess the Muslim religion, speak the Malay language and conform to Malay customs.

11 Malays are also identified with the *bumiputra* – literally, sons of the soil – to whom special privileges have been extended since the 1970s; all Malays are *bumiputra*, but not all *bumiputra* are Malay, especially in eastern Malaysia.

12 See Anne Katherine Larsen, 'The Impact of the Islamic Resurgence on the Belief System of Rural Malays', *Temenos*, 32 (1996), pp. 137–54.

13 Hussin Mutalib, *Islam in Malaysia: From Revivalism to Islamic State?* (Singapore: Singapore University Press, 1993), p. 34.

14 Leonard Sebastian, 'Values and Governance Issues in the Foreign Policy of Singapore', in Han Sung-Joo (ed.), *Changing Values in Asia* (Tokyo and New York: Japan Center for International Exchange, 1999), p. 229.

15 See Iik Arifin Mansurnoor, 'Islam in Brunei Darussalam and Global Islam', in Meuleman (ed.), *Islam in the Era of Globalization*, pp. 71–98.

16 *Ibid.*, pp. 82–83.

17 There is a small number of Shi'ites in the provinces of Lanao del Sur and Zamboanga del Sur.

18 Peter Gowing, *Muslim Filipinos – Heritage and Horizon* (Quezon City: New Day Publishers, 1979), pp. 9-10.

19 'The Diverse Culture of Mindanao', www.seasite.niu.edu/Tagalog/Mindanao/Mindanao_Culture/mindanao_culture.htm.

20 Peter Gowing, 'How Muslim Are the Muslim Filipinos?', cited in Jacqueline Siapno, 'Balkik-Islam (Islamic Resurgence) in Muslim Mindanao', *Maganda*, Autumn 1991, www.magandamagazine.org.

21 'Islamic Resurgence as an International Movement', in *ibid*.

22 Gowing, *Muslim Filipinos*, pp. 70–71.

23 *Ibid.*, p. 86.

24 David Buchman, Report on Faculty International Study Travel Program, Thailand, 2000, ahrens.hanover.edu/fdc/Reports/Buchman-Fist2000.htm.

25 *Ibid.*

26 Claudia Canesso, *Cambodia* (Philadelphia, PA: Chelsea House Publishers, 1999), pp. 63, 75; cited in www.adherents.com/Na_325.html.

27 The Cham's roots lie in the ancient Kingdom of Champa, which once extended through south and central Vietnam.

28 Luke Hunt, 'Cambodia's Muslim Culture Shifting Toward Fundamentalism', *AFP*, 27 October 2002.

29 *The World Factbook, Burma*
(Washington DC: Central
Intelligence Agency, 2002).
See also the sources cited in
www.adherents.com/Na_335.html
under Islam/Myanmar.

30 Human Rights Watch,
'Background on Muslims in
Burma', *Human Rights Brief*,
July 2002.

31 *Ibid.*

32 Maung Maung Oo, 'Terror in
America, Backlash in Burma',
The Irrawaddy, vol. 9, no. 8,
October–November 2001.

33 Azra, 'Globalization of
Indonesian Muslim Discourse',
in Meuleman (ed.), *Islam in the
Era of Globalization*, pp. 40–42.

Chapter 2

1 Pancasila means 'five principles':
belief in (1) the One and Only God;
(2) a just and civilised humanity;
(3) the unity of Indonesia;
(4) democracy; and (5) social justice.

2 International Crisis Group (ICG),
'Al-Qaeda in Southeast Asia: The
Case of the "Ngruki Network" in
Indonesia', *Indonesia Briefing*,
8 August 2002, pp. 3–4.

3 Following the fall of Suharto and
the lifting of controls on political
activity, the PPP has returned to
an Islam-based ideology.

4 Muhamad Hisyam, 'The
Interaction of Religion and State
in Indonesia', in Meuleman (ed.),
Islam in the Era of Globalization,
pp. 308–12.

5 Azra, 'Globalization of
Indonesian Muslim Discourse',
in Meuleman (ed.), *Islam in the
Era of Globalization*, pp. 36–37.

6 KISDI sponsored activities in
support of the Bosnian Muslims.
Funds were raised through the
National Committee for
Solidarity with the Bosnian
Muslims, chaired by Suharto's
stepbrother; see 'Indonesia
Alert!', January 2001,
www.indonesiaalert.org/index.html.

7 Azra, 'Globalization of
Indonesian Muslim Discourse',
in Meuleman (ed.), *Islam in the
Era of Globalization*, p. 34. For an
overview of Suharto's tactical
turn towards Islam in the 1990s,
see Michael Vatikiotis, *Indonesian
Politics Under Suharto* (London
and New York: Routledge, 1993),
pp. 132–38.

8 Michael Davis, 'Laskar Jihad and
the Political Position of
Conservative Islam in Indonesia',
Contemporary Southeast Asia,
vol. 24, no. 1, April 2002, p. 28.

9 In a press interview in which he
proclaimed the 'death of
ideology', Muhammadiyah
chairman Ahmad Syafii Maarif
scorned the idea of an Islamic
state; '"Ideology Is Dead" in
Politics'.

10 'Muslim Leaders Slam Militants'
Arrest', *Straits Times* (Singapore),
8 January 2002.

11 United States–Indonesia Society
(USINDO), 'Parliamentary
Elections in Indonesia: Consensus,
Coalition, or Confusion?',
Proceedings of USINDO
Workshop, Washington DC,
22 June 1999, pp. 10–16.

12 Interview with Ulil Abshar
Abdalla, Jakarta, June 2002.

13 Discussion with leaders of the
Justice Party, Jakarta, June 2002.
There are those who believe that
the party is controlled by a
clandestine inner circle of more
radical leaders, and that its real
agenda is radical Islamisation.

14 Presentation by Dr Michael Taylor,
'Turbulent Times Past and Present
in the Moluccas', USINDO Open
Forum, Washington DC, 13
September 2000.

15 See Angel Rabasa and Peter
Chalk, *Indonesia's Transformation
and the Stability of Southeast Asia*,
MR-1344-AF (Santa Monica, CA:
RAND, 2000), pp. 41–44.

16 Presentation by Indonesian
Ambassador Dorodjatun
Kuntjoro-Jakti, USINDO Open

Forum, Washington DC, 21 July 2000; Rabasa and Chalk, *Indonesia's Transformation*, p. 44.

17 ICG, 'Indonesia Backgrounder: How the Jemaah Islamiyah Terrorist Network Operates', *ICG Asia Report 43* (Jakarta/Brussels: 11 December 2002), pp. 22–23.

18 ICG, 'Indonesia: The Search for Peace in Maluku', 8 February 2002, pp. 13–14.

19 'The Conflict in Central Sulawesi', Program on Humanitarian Policy and Conflict Research, Harvard College, www.preventconflict.org/portal/main/maps_sulawesi_conflict.php.

20 Ayip Syafruddin, 'Why Laskar Jihad Is Heading to Poso', laskarjihad.or.id/english/article/headingtoposo.htm.

21 Michael Davis, 'Laskar Jihad and the Political Position of Conservative Islam in Indonesia', *Contemporary Southeast Asia*, vol. 24, no. 1, April 2002, p. 23.

22 Interview with Ulil Abshar-Abdalla, Jakarta, June 2002.

23 Marcus Mietzner, 'Nationalism and Islamic Politics: Political Islam in the Post-Suharto Era', in Budiman et al. (eds), *Reformasi*, p. 183.

24 At least one of Megawati's closest advisers warned about the risks of not confronting the extremists sooner rather than later. Discussions with senior Indonesian government and intelligence officials, Jakarta, February 2002.

25 ICG, 'Indonesia: The Search for Peace in Maluku', p. 16.

26 'Hand of Terror: Key Suspects Prepare To Face the Music', *Straits Times*, 20 September 2002.

27 Zachary Abuza, 'Tentacles of Terror: Al-Qaeda's Southeast Asia Network', unpublished manuscript, 21 November 2002, p. 50.

28 Correspondence with Derwin Pereira, the *Straits Times*' Jakarta correspondent, December 2002.

29 'Suicide Bomber Blew Up Paddy's Club in Kuta', *Tempo Interactive*, 22 November 2002.

30 Correspondence with Derwin Pereira, December 2002.

31 'Muslim Organizations Back Antiterrorist Regulations', *Jakarta Post*, 21 October 2002.

32 'National Police Arrests Imam Samudera AKA Kudama', *Tempo*, 21 November 2002.

33 Bashir was also charged with breaking the laws on the possession of firearms and explosives and destruction of property. If convicted, he could face the death penalty.

34 'Indonesian Arrest of Muslim Cleric Raises Criticism', *Wall Street Journal*, 21 October 2002.

35 'VP Denies Govt Interference in the Arrest of Bashir', *Jakarta Post*, 22 October 2002.

36 ICG, *Indonesia Backgrounder*, p 5. The ICG does not identify the source of its information.

37 Political activist George Aditjondro alleges that the Laskar Jihad's operations in Maluku were financed by Yayasan Amal Bhakti Pancasila, one of Suharto's charitable foundations, and by associates of former President Habibie. 'Financing Human Rights Violations in Indonesia (I)', Indonesia Alert, Autumn 2001, www.indonesiaalert.org/Articles/01-02/Aditjondro.htm.

38 Barry Desker, *Islam and Society in Southeast Asia After September 11* (Singapore: Institute of Defence and Strategic Studies, September 2002), p. 8.

39 See Angel Rabasa and John Haseman, *The Military and Democracy in Indonesia: Challenges, Politics and Power*, MR-SRF-1599 (Santa Monica, CA: RAND), 2002, pp. 61–67.

Chapter 3

1 Muzaffar, *Islamic Resurgence in Malaysia*, pp. 50–52.

[2] These included late PAS president Fadzil Noor, Abdul Hadi Awang, Nakhaie Ahmad and Syed Ibrahim Rahman.

[3] Farish A Noor, 'Ustaz Haji Yusuf bin Abdullah al-Rawa: Architect of the "New PAS" of the 1980s', pasjt.tripod.com/a/saf/yusuf_rawa.htm.

[4] Muzaffar, *Islamic Resurgence in Malaysia*, p. 85.

[5] *Ibid.*, pp. 78–82.

[6] 'Malaysia a "Fundamentalist" Islamic Country, Says PM', *Malaysiakini*, 17 June 2002.

[7] Mark L. Clifford and Pete Engardio, *Meltdown: Asia's Boom, Bust, and Beyond* (Upper Saddle River, NJ: Prentice Hall, 2000), p. 227.

[8] Roger Mitton, 'Showing Who Is Boss: The PM Boldly Settles a Couple of Old Scores', *Asiaweek*, 17 May 1996.

[9] John Funston, 'Malaysia's Tenth Elections: Status Quo, Reformasi, or Islamization?' *Contemporary Southeast Asia*, vol. 22, no. 1, April 2000, pp. 50–56.

[10] Mutalib, *Islam in Malaysia*, pp. 86–88.

[11] 'Mid-East Groups Attend PAS Forum', *Straits Times*, 30 May 2002.

[12] Interview with PAS Member of Parliament Syed Azman Syed Ahmad, Kuala Lumpur, May 2002.

[13] S. Jayasankaran, 'A Plan to End Extremism', *Far Eastern Economic Review*, 26 December 2002–2 January 2003.

[14] See tables 7.1 to 7.4 in Raj Vasil, *Governing Singapore: A History of National Development and Democracy* (St Leonards: Allen & Unwin, 2000), pp. 222–23.

[15] 'Latest on Hijab Issue', *Fateha*, 28 March 2002; 'Morality Vs School Uniform Policy', *ibid.*, 24 April 2002, www.fateha.com.

[16] Government of Singapore, Press Release on ISA Arrests, December 2001; see also Government of Singapore, 'The Jemaah Islamiyah Arrests and the Threat of Terrorism', January 2003, Annex C.

Chapter 4

[1] This is also the title of an important collection of essays on social, economic and political conditions in Mindanao: Mark Turner, R. J. May and Respall Lulu Turner (eds), *Mindanao: Land of Unfulfilled Promise* (Quezon City: New Day Publishers, 1992).

[2] Vic Hurley, 'Swish of the Kris: The Story of the Moros', www.bakbakan.com/swishk/swk2-14.html.

[3] R. J. May, 'The Wild West in the South: A Recent Political History of Mindanao', in Turner, May and Respall Turner (eds), *Mindanao*, pp. 125–26.

[4] Fred Hill, 'Ethnic Cleansing in Mindanao, Philippines. Islamic Horizons', 17 April 1996, www.hartford-hwp.com/archives/54a/015.html.

[5] See Gowing, *Muslim Filipinos*, pp. 212–18.

[6] See 'Salamat Hashim Speaks: The Muslim Separatist Leader Wants "the East Timor Formula"', *Asiaweek*, vol. 26, no. 12, 31 March 2000.

[7] Sayyid Qutb, the most important ideologue of the Islamic revolution since Hasan al-Banna, was executed by the Egyptian government in 1966. Mawdudi, the founder of the Jamaat-i-Islamiyah, an influential Pakistani *dakwah* organisation, was sentenced to death for militant activities in Pakistan in 1953, but received an amnesty. He died in exile in the US in 1979.

[8] See 'MILF Leader to "Nida'ul Islam": Perhaps the Moro Struggle for Freedom and Self-Determination is the Longest and Bloodiest in the Entire History of Mankind', *Nida'ul Islam*,

www.islam.org.au/articles/23/ph2.htm, April–May 1998.

9   Peter Chalk, 'Muslim Separatist Movements in the Philippines and Thailand', in Angel and Chalk (eds), *Indonesia's Transformation*, pp. 84–90; and Abuza, 'Tentacles of Terror', p. 17.

10   Christos Iacovou, 'From MNLF to Abu Sayyaf: The Radicalization of Islam in the Philippines', www.ict.org.il/articles/articledet.cfm?articleid=116, 11 July 2000.

11   See Abuza, 'Tentacles of Terror', pp. 13–20.

12   Government of Singapore, 'The Jemaah Islamiyah Arrests', p. 8.

13   Daniel Joseph Ringuet, 'The Continuation of Civil Unrest and Poverty in Mindanao', *Contemporary Southeast Asia*, vol. 24, no. 1, April 2002, pp. 40–41.

14   May, 'The Wild West in the South', in Turner, May and Respall Turner (eds), *Mindanao*, pp. 135–36.

15   Ringuet, 'The Continuation of Civil Unrest', p. 43.

16   Amina Rasul, 'A Look at Corruption in the ARMM and the Role of Faith-Based Organizations in Fighting Corruption', unpublished manuscript, 2001.

17   Mel C. Labrador, 'The Philippines in 2001', *Asian Survey*, vol. 42, no. 1, p. 147.

18   Fe B. Zamora, 'Al Harakatul al Islamiya: The Beginnings of Abu Sayyaf', www.inq7.net/specials/inside_abusayyaf/2001/features.htm, 2001.

19   See Rabasa and Chalk, *Indonesia's Transformation*, pp. 88–92.

20   Zamora, 'Al Harakatul al Islamiya'.

21   'Janjalani Brothers Ask To Talk Peace', *Inquirer News Service*, Manila, 21 June 2001.

22   Cited in Ringuet, 'The Continuation of Civil Unrest', p. 44.

23   US forces were not to engage in operations, but the rules of engagement permitted them to fire in self-defence.

24   Videoconference with Defense Secretary Angelo Reyes, RAND, Santa Monica, CA, 15 August 2002.

25   'GMA: Crush Abu Sayyaf in 90 Days', *Manila Times*, 1 March 2003.

26   Labrador, 'The Philippines in 2001', p. 146.

27   'MILF Kills 14 in Rampage', *Manila Times*, 21 February 2003.

28   'Manila Police Link Davao Airport Blast to MILF', *Straits Times*, 8 March 2003.

29   Peter Chalk, 'Thailand', in Jason Isaacson and Colin Rubenstein (eds), *Islam in Asia: Changing Political Realities* (Washington DC and Melbourne: AJC and AIJAC, 1999), p. 166.

30   See Peter Chalk, 'Political Terrorism in Southeast Asia', *Terrorism and Political Violence*, vol. 10, no. 2, 1998; 'Chronology of Southern Violence', *Bangkok Post*, 1 February 1998.

31   'PM: Peace in South Vital to Growth Triangle', *Bangkok Post*, 21 January 1998.

32   '50 Southern Separatists Surrender', *ibid.*, 12 March 1998; 'Southern Rebels Surrender' and 'Southern Rebels Meet Deadline to Surrender', *ibid.*, 10 March 1998.

33   'Separatists in Malaysia Flee Abroad', *ibid.*, 22 February 1998; 'Separatists Flee "Haven"', *ibid.*, 26 February 1998.

34   Surin Pitsuwan, *Islam and Malay Nationalism: A Case Study of the Malay-Muslims of Southern Thailand* (Bangkok: Thai Khadi Research Institute, Thammasat University, 1985).

35   Peter Searle, 'Ethno-Religious Conflicts: Rise or Decline? Recent Developments in Southeast Asia', *Contemporary Southeast Asia*, vol. 24, no. 1, April 2002, pp. 7–8.

36   Peter Chalk, *Grey Area Phenomena in Southeast Asia: Piracy, Drug*

Trafficking and Political Terrorism (Canberra: Strategic and Defence Studies Centre, Australian National University, 1997), p. 62; 'Ties of Faith', *Far Eastern Economic Review*, 11 April 1996.

Chapter 5

1   Sources for this chapter are government and intelligence sources in Malaysia, Indonesia and Singapore, as well as extensive coverage in the regional media. Of particular interest are the reports by Derwin Pereira, the *Straits Times* correspondent in Jakarta (see 'Is There an Al-Qaeda Connection in Indonesia?' *Sunday Times Singapore*, 20 January 2002); and by Leslie Lopez and Jay Solomon in *The Asian Wall Street Journal* (see 'Indonesia Cleric Becomes Focus of Terror Manhunt', *AWSJ*, 1–3 February 2002). See also Rohan Gunaratna, 'Al-Qaeda: The Asian Connection', *Straits Times*, 4 January 2002; and the detailed coverage in the Jakarta weekly *Tempo*, 29 January–4 February 2002. Two important documents are also available. Zachary Abuza, 'Tentacles of Terror: Al-Qaeda's Southeast Asian Network', based on his forthcoming book, *Terrorism and Radical Islam in Southeast Asia* (Boulder, CO: Lynne Rienner Publishers, 2003); and the Singapore government's White Paper 'The Jemaah Islamiyah Arrests and the Threat of Terrorism', 7 January 2003.

2   Abuza, 'Tentacles of Terror', pp. 41–45.

3   According to the *Straits Times*, between 1997 and 2002 Jemaah Islamiyah received 1.35 billion Indonesian rupiah ($135,000) from al-Qaeda. Indonesian intelligence believes that the amount is even higher than this. See Pereira, 'Is There an Al-Qaeda

Connection in Indonesia?'.

4   Government of Singapore, Press Release on ISA Arrests; and 'The Jemaah Islamiyah Arrests and the Threat of Terrorism', pp. 10–15 and Annexes A and C.

5   Leslie Lopez, 'Portrait of a Radical Network in Asia', *Wall Street Journal*, 13 August 2002.

6   Abuza, 'Tentacles of Terror', p. 59.

7   *Ibid*. See also the chart in Government of Singapore, 'The Jemaah Islamiyah Arrests and the Threat of Terrorism', p. 10.

8   'Web of Terror: Jemaah Islamiah Forged Links with Regional Groups'; and 'Govt Reveals Plot to Spark Religious Violence Here', *Straits Times*, 20 September 2002.

9   'Looking for SE Asia's Own Carlos the Jackal', *Jakarta Post*, 30 January 2002.

10   Derwin Pereira, 'Is There an Al-Qaeda Connection in Indonesia?', *Sunday (Straits) Times*, 20 January 2002, p. 35.

11   See ICG, 'Al-Qaeda in Southeast Asia'.

12   *Ibid.*, p. 7; Lopez, 'Portrait of a Radical Network'.

13   Abuza, 'Tentacles of Terror', p. 53.

14   ICG, 'Al-Qaeda in Southeast Asia', pp. 10–12, 16.

15   'Philippines Jails Indonesian Linked to Al-Qaeda', *Laksmana.net*, 12 July 2002.

16   Romesh Ratnesar, 'Confessions of an Al-Qaeda Terrorist', *Time*, 23 September 2002.

17   'JI Militants May Have Links with Separatist Group', Straits Times, 18 September 2002; 'Indonesian Arrested in Manila Had Ties to al-Qaeda', *Washington Post*, 9 May 2002.

18   Abuza, 'Tentacles of Terror', p. 54.

19   'Indonesian Cleric Becomes Focus of Terror Manhunt', *Asian Wall Street Journal*, 1–3 February 2002; Abuza, 'Tentacles of Terror', pp. 23–27.

20   Abuza, 'Tentacles of Terror', pp. 27–29.

21   For details on Rohman al-

Ghozi's background and the charges against him, see *Tempo*, 29 January–4 February 2002.

22 'Manila Nabs "Supplier of Singapore-bound Explosives"', *Straits Times*, 10 July 2002.

23 'Web of Terror: Jemaah Islamiah Forged Links with Regional Groups', *ibid.*, 20 September 2002.

24 Ratnesar, 'Confessions of an Al-Qaeda Terrorist'.

25 'Manila Suspends Talks with Rebel Group After Allegations of Its Links to al-Qaeda', *Wall Street Journal*, 12 March 2002.

26 'ASEAN To Step Up Efforts with US in War on Terrorism', *International Herald Tribune*, 31 July 2002.

Conclusion

1 'Powell in Jakarta: US To Give Indonesia $50 Million to Fight Terror', *Reuters*, 2 August 2002; 'Powell Says US Ready for Expanded Military Ties with Indonesia', *AFP*, 2 August 2002.

2 Council on Foreign Relations, 'Terrorism: Q&A', www.terrorismanswers.com/responses/diplomacy_print.html, 2003; Statement by Charlotte Beers, Undersecretary of State for Public Diplomacy, Hearing before the US Senate Committee on Foreign Relations, 27 February 2003.

3 Rabasa and Haseman, *The Military and Democracy in Indonesia*.

4 Rasul, 'A Look at Corruption in the ARMM'.

5 I am indebted for this information to Nancy Yuan, Vice-President and Director of the Washington Office of the Asia Foundation. The Asia Foundation provides assistance to civil-society groups in Southeast Asia.

6 See Robert W. Hefner, *Civil Islam: Muslims and Democratization in Indonesia* (Princeton, NJ: Princeton University Press, 2000).